The Service Organization

PERSPECTIVES ON BUSINESS

Series editor: Professor Diane Coyle

Why You Dread Work: What's Going Wrong in Your Workplace and How to Fix It — Helen Holmes

Digital Transformation at Scale: Why the Strategy Is Delivery (Second Edition) — Andrew Greenway, Ben Terrett, Mike Bracken and Tom Loosemore

The Service Organization: How to Deliver and Lead Successful Services, Sustainably — Kate Tarling

The Service Organization
How to Deliver and Lead Successful Services, Sustainably

Kate Tarling

LONDON PUBLISHING PARTNERSHIP

Published by London Publishing Partnership
www.londonpublishingpartnership.co.uk

Published in association with
Enlightenment Economics
www.enlightenmenteconomics.com

ISBN: 978-1-913019-76-1 (pbk)
ISBN: 978-1-913019-77-8 (iPDF)
ISBN: 978-1-913019-78-5 (epub)

A catalogue record for this book is
available from the British Library

This book has been composed in Candara

Copy-edited and typeset by
T&T Productions Ltd, London
www.tandtproductions.com

Printed and bound in Great Britain
by Page Bros

Contents

CONTENTS

Foreword

I'm a longtime fan of Kate Tarling and her holistic, practical advice for improving services at scale. If you've followed her work, there's a theme: to modernize services, it's the underlying organizational working practices that need to be transformed for teams to be successful.

In 2017, she and Ayesha Moarif gave an unforgettable presentation called 'The actual problems to be solved'. I was hooked from the moment I saw the title. The talk featured the following seemingly straightforward problem statement:

> We need a portal for applicants to submit their bank statements electronically.

If you've worked on a digital team, you've probably been asked to build something similar. What followed was a slide I've shared with team after team over the years, turning that simple statement on its head. Calling out each part of that sentence, they asked:

- What are users trying to do?
- Who is 'we'?
- Why now? Or else?
- Why this? How else?
- Why do users need this?
- What does this data tell us?
- What does this allow us to do?

Pausing to answer each of those questions makes you reframe the problem based on the outcome users need, not what a department or programme needs. By questioning each assumption in that statement, Kate and Ayesha taught us to realize that services exist to help people accomplish something. And great services explore (and deliver on) what users are trying to do, not just what the service provider needs from them.

However, the truly brilliant part of the talk was the deep dive that followed – examples, case studies, tips and practical tools to help teams accomplish the goal of getting from assumptions and ideas to outcomes and focusing on what the service needs to achieve. Kate follows this same playbook in her book, pairing her extensive knowledge with real-world examples that bring the work to life. This practical 'how-to' approach, based on Kate's decades of experience working with teams navigating organizational change, means you can put her words into instant action. Each chapter contains in-depth, tactical information to guide you at any stage of your transformation journey.

After twenty-five years working in and around governments, large and small, state and federal, in both the United States and Canada, I can deeply relate to the culture shifts that must accompany modernization. I lived through the evolution of 'e-government' from fillable PDFs, replicating paper forms on the internet, and many requests for portals to today's more user-centred, service design approach.

Over the last decade, I've had the privilege of helping create 18F, a digital service team inside the US federal government, and the Ontario Digital Service in Ontario, Canada. These teams, like the US Digital Service, the UK Government Digital Service and digital service teams around the world, are working hard to make it easier for people to interact with their governments – from ordering free COVID-19 tests to modernizing health care, student aid or immigration systems. They're building the foundational platforms and services to give people the seamless experience they expect in a connected age. Yet I suspect their lasting impact will not be the services themselves but the behavioural and cultural changes that are creating the conditions for excellent delivery. Beyond technology and tools, these teams are embedding how they deliver into the fabric of their organization's practices and processes.

As someone who has now spent the last several years building teams instead of services, I gobbled up page after page of this book, highlighting entire sections to send to senior executives I know. Kate's written *the* manual for any leader or team to reinvent their organization by putting successful services – i.e. successful users – at the heart of how it operates.

Just as Microsoft CEO Satya Nadella reminded us that 'every company is a software company', Kate reminds us that every organization is a service organization. But too often our companies, structures and teams aren't set up to deliver whole, human-centred services. This book is a play-by-play for any organization, division or team working to deliver services at scale. Whether you're leading a huge organization or, like me, are working to amplify ideas from a smaller experiment, *The Service Organization* will teach you how everyone in your organization can contribute to improving the services they provide to their users.

Start from the beginning, or jump into any chapter, and you'll be on your way to understanding 'the actual problems to be solved'.

Hillary Hartley, Digital Government Leader
Toronto, Ontario, Canada

Preface

M any books offer advice for designing new services or introducing modern ways of developing them. They often focus on one individual service or team. What about large organizations with dozens of teams and hundreds of services?

Instead of searching for the ideal process, if you don't have the right conditions, you need to focus on creating them first. Doing anything else is futile.

Services help people to do or to achieve something, while delivering an outcome for the provider. Service providers include insurance, banking and finance, retail, telecoms, utilities, transport, tourism, entertainment and many technology companies, as well as governments and not-for-profits.

In large organizations most services already exist – they just don't work how you would design them today. Services have too often come to reflect the internal structure of the organization itself. And these organizations aren't designed in a way that results in joined-up services that do the job we need them to do. While teams change or modernize individual parts, it's usually a disjointed and discontinuous effort, and this limits how well services work, how efficient they are to operate, and how well they deliver outcomes for the organization.

There are many different ways organizations and industries think about who they serve. Throughout the book I refer to *users* or *people*, by which I also mean humans, citizens, customers, patients, buyers, claimants, clients and businesses (in the case of organizations that serve other businesses).

Why this book exists

This is the book I wish someone could have handed to me when I began to work with very large organizations. I wrote a series of practical blog posts on how to improve services at scale. These resonated with tens of thousands of people from every professional discipline. I've since worked with dozens of large organizations across hundreds of services. I've interviewed executives, board members and practitioners. The ideas I present have been developed and refined with the contribution of many others. I've taught hundreds of practitioners and executives at world-class institutions. The ideas in this book are a product of decades of research, as well as hands-on experience.

One aim of the book is to change the conversation so that it's not about trying to persuade others to think more like you do. Instead, it arms you with evidence and arguments that give a compelling reason to change; that is, to solve problems that people are already struggling with. Much of what's in this book applies the underlying principles of modern approaches, but it does so in a way that doesn't exclude people.

It gives you the practical skills, tools and knowledge to bring sense and clarity to chaos, so that everyone has a clear path to create true service organizations, including handling the necessary conversations along the way.

What this book covers

This book is a guide for how to turn even the most traditional of companies into more successful service organizations. It will help redefine organizations in terms of services from the perspective of the people that need them. It shows how to shape and steer the work of teams towards improving those services and how to evaluate and measure service performance in a way that brings everyone together: practitioners, operations, strategy and policy. It provides new approaches for service measurement, governance and accountability, programme structures, leadership and strategy.

It contains dozens of real-life practical examples, which haven't been shared before, from the organizations, teams and individuals doing the work to deliver better services at scale.

It's been said that in some books, the advice can feel like your house is on fire while someone shows you a house that isn't on fire and tells you to make yours more like that.[1] Sometimes, you'll be told in detail about methods in companies that had the benefit of designing it all from scratch in the last ten years. Instead, this book addresses the reality of how large organizations operate today. It turns the challenge of delivering high-performing services into a series of solvable puzzles. Sometimes it's a game of chess. It's worth playing the game because these large organizations are the ones that bring the opportunity to improve services at an enormous scale and in some of the most important areas affecting our lives.

Each chapter looks at a major problem that organizations need to solve, with practical ideas for what to do about it, and in ways that result in more successful services by default. The hard thing isn't knowing how to design better individual services, but rather changing the conditions inside organizations so everyone else can improve services consistently. It provides the scaffolding that you need to put together in the organizations you work with, and it shows what you yourself can do to create the conditions needed for better services – starting this week.

This book is full of practical guidance for how to transform service-providing organizations. It's not a complete list of every tactic or scenario you might encounter. There will be many conditions that are unique to your context or domain. But I hope the ideas here provide a good place to start that will save you time and energy, and that you can adapt and evolve.

Introduction

An organization is either orienting itself to make better services or it isn't.

Every industry is becoming a service industry. Every government is a service provider.

Apple used to just make Macs; much of its business now is subscription-based services like music or TV.[1] Ford used to just build cars; now the focus is on getting people and goods from A to B with tools to support delivery services.[2] It used to take several months to get a passport; in the UK you can now apply online, with your own digital photo, and a passport can be delivered to your house just a few days later. Even coffee has become a service.

But larger, older organizations aren't structured to deliver services seamlessly, from beginning to end – not in a way that helps people do what they need or want to do successfully, or to get the best outcome. Most were never designed as service organizations. They don't even operate as single organizations, but as collections of different functions. This is a barrier to making services successful because they often cut across an organization and its functions. Changing how a service works in one insurance firm today might involve fifteen different leadership teams, delivery teams, project management offices, directorates, governing bodies and planning functions – and that's before we consider the policyholders, the agents, the wider industry and the regulators.

As a result, the way large organizations view service performance is in pieces – and from the inside. Organizations don't use their own services. Not as a whole. Not in all the situations that people are in. They don't see how they perform in real life or what the resulting impact is for the organization. They might have a 'voice of customer' team, but in one government department that means measuring satisfaction directly *after* someone submits an application. What this doesn't show is that people confidently apply for the wrong thing in the first place.

We rely on services every day to do the important things in life: getting to work, buying a house, seeking treatment for a health condition, or paying the right amount of tax. A service helps someone to do or to achieve something, while delivering an outcome for the organization providing that service.

A service includes everything involved, from beginning to end and top to bottom. EE provides mobile phone, landline and internet services.[3] Getting a new phone line involves everything the customer sees and interacts with, including the website, the contact centre and the engineer who visits. It's the rules and regulations for the service, such as needing to be over 18 years old to receive it. And it's also everything behind the scenes, including the technology behind the appointment booking, the data integration needed to establish property location, the systems used to support the management of customer records, as well as tools to measure overall performance. Significantly improving the performance of a large service like this is about much more than just the design of an app.

When individual parts of a large service are changed without an understanding of the whole, problems are created. One such problem is how well staff are supported. Internal staff have to use the tools we give them to help customers. Joy is a frontline staff member for an airline.[4] Each time the internal system is upgraded it gets harder to use, not easier. The people who bought the expensive internal system in the first place are far removed from the staff who have to use it. They don't see how it's slower, less accurate and less joined up when Joy helps people to book or change flights.

Typical structures in large organizations mean that different functions provide different parts of a service. Other teams make decisions about changing and modernizing those parts. These arrangements dictate how well services perform overall. When services don't work well, that results in extra cost, time, friction, effort, errors, rework, delays and confusion for everyone. This usually generates more work and it costs organizations more to operate, as more people need to contact them, or do the wrong things, or fail to do what's needed.

But bad services aren't just more expensive. They have real human costs too. They stop people getting the outcomes they need. They prevent organizations from fulfilling their purpose. Eve suffers from eight different medical conditions. It's a full-time job to navigate the clinical system and make it to specialist appointments. There are hand-offs between organizations, departments and individuals. This means that Eve often has to start from scratch, or has the wrong letter, or that the people she sees don't have the right information to help her. Kind but overworked clinicians spend more time trying to connect and chase things up for her.

Addressing the problem

There are three parts to creating a clear path forward.

Part 1. Turn from inside-out to outside-in

Organizations need to put the emphasis on what customers and users need or what they want to do or achieve. This means redefining what they offer in terms of services as their users would think of them.

Many organizations would say they already know their customers and their services. Yet they only view the problems

3

and the opportunities through the lens of their existing products and processes.[5] The default approach is discontinuous improvement, and efforts to change are disjointed, whether it is replacing technology, publishing PDFs, procuring a contract, rearranging how data is formatted and stored, or implementing 'enterprise' software. These are only single pieces of the puzzle. The connection often isn't made between this work and how it impacts service performance or changes what works for people inside and out, which means no one is there to keep the work on the right path for the outcomes the organization needs.

The drive for change should be improving whole services, using performance in the real world to determine what needs to change internally – and how.

Part 2. Existing conditions get the existing results

Instead of spending your time tackling problems for an individual project or service, you can amplify your influence by changing the culture and processes responsible for how things work today. Nobody will ask you to do this, but it's the only way for everyone to be able to create better services by default.

If services aren't working well, that's a result of current processes, governance, relationships and decision-making.[6] If you were creating an organization from scratch to make successful services today, you wouldn't separate all the people who need to work together, but many of the problems with services are hidden by the default ways in which large organizations work. Solving these problems is very valuable.

Services are changing. This is partly because of opportunities and risks posed by the internet and technology. The recent pandemic showed many organizations that they can work without a building, but if a website or app is broken they can't function at all. Many organizations were already making parts of their services more digital, which creates a faster feedback loop between users and the organization. If the team publishing guidance to the NHS website includes a sentence that confuses everyone, it immediately drives calls to GPs' surgeries. If it then takes a committee three weeks to agree how to change that sentence when 100,000 people are calling their doctor, the service will sink. It damages people's trust.

We know how to establish multidisciplinary teams who deliver, while demonstrating the value of modern ways of working, but we haven't had effective ways of modernizing at scale across entire organizations. To improve how services perform across the entire organization sustainably, changes to team structure, leadership, governance, planning and working practices are required.

Part 3. Orient the organization around its services

What customers and users actually need and do doesn't change much over time – unless the purpose of the service provider does. Their expectations about how well organizations serve their needs may change. Orient organizations to anticipate and address problems and opportunities for external users as the basis for driving internal change. It's a timeless and more sustainable way of operating. Everything else about how we choose to serve people and address opportunities changes much more often, from design to processes, to internal systems and data. Anchoring these changes to the end result is a safer and more realistic way to set them up for success.

People need to agree on *what good looks like* if they are going to be able to work together towards it. What it looks like to be a true service organization, with capabilities and processes in place that allow the organization to learn and to iterate what they do; moving away from separate functions, teams and individuals acting independently towards working as a whole, across the whole.

The right conditions

Rather than power and ownership, this model entails *guardianship*: a culture of individuals who care about the whole and not just their own part, who place value on working together and who are open to learning from one another.

That's because making successful services involves all the decisions and the set-up behind the scenes. It's about how we arrange the parts and how they work together, and from where an organization draws its impetus to change.

Creating the conditions for everyone else to make better services includes doing the following.

- The organization evaluating and measuring its services and making itself interested in and accountable for their performance.
- Enabling functions (such as finance, legal, commercial or procurement) working to support service teams to do what's most valuable.
- Choosing the right type and combination of the parts that users see, and designing them to work well.
- Having clarity of vision in order to drive whole service improvement in line with priorities.
- Choosing and creating the right technology and processes. Being able to iterate these supporting capabilities within sensible parameters.
- Guiding research so that teams understand the reality of people and situations. Structuring insight for the current priorities while anticipating the future.
- Governance processes that propagate the right kind of work to improve services and that keep it on the right path, taking into account the reality of users, strategy or policy, operations, capability building and deliverability.
- Protecting and unblocking teams that deliver valuable change, and aligning work across the organization for more successful services.

Every one of these components is at the sharp end of an organization's performance. Yet organizations often leave this to simply 'happen' – or worse, their default approach actually works against it. Choices about how these foundations work has an impact on how successful our services are. How to set them up isn't a matter of preference for an individual leader to decide alone, or a management fad to follow.

Some organizations provide one service; others provide hundreds. Some provide one part of a service or help others to provide services. Whether the organization you work with already sees it that way or not, the guidance in this book will help you set the stage for better services by default.

How to change the conditions

An organization won't 'want' to change how it operates, especially if the problems and costs of the status quo aren't visible. The culture will only change if the cost of not changing is too high.

But the stimulus to change cannot be separate from the people, culture and processes that need to change. For people to work together there has to be a genuinely mutually agreed model for modernization that focuses on services. That starts with finding the right people to work with, whatever their background or discipline, and addressing together each problem that gets in the way.

You don't need to force others to learn new words or methodologies to create the right conditions. It should feel simple and sensible to everyone who cares about the organization's users, goals, operations and outcomes, and to everyone who wants to make more successful services. When it feels obvious to others after the fact, who now wouldn't want to work any other way, it means you've changed the conditions successfully and sustainably across the organization.

Creating service organizations that deliver successful services by default can be a radical change. It might seem daunting. It can threaten power structures. You may not have the remit or the permission, but nobody else will either. This book breaks it down into simple, useful and achievable tasks that you are perfectly well set up to do and that will win the support of others as you go. It's vital to the success of service organizations to do this. Enormous opportunities lie ahead. It's also a good way to improve the lives and livelihoods of the people and businesses who rely on services.

Chapter 1

Redefine your organization by the services it provides

Organizations don't see themselves in terms of services as their customers and users would think of them. The focus is often on organizational structure, internal functions, processes and technology. When you join somewhere new, you're more likely to be shown the 'org chart' than the services to people.

How an organization arranges itself likely won't match what users need, expect or want to do. And this results in services that cost more to run, don't work well and don't deliver the intended outcomes. These problems are often invisible because organizations aren't looking at what gets in the way – and they therefore don't see the extent to which their default working practices are the cause.

Our goal is to help organizations see themselves differently and begin to judge their performance by how well services work in the real world. A good place to start is to look at what users are trying to do or what outcome they need. A service includes everything involved in delivering that outcome. Defining services this way means you can assess how well they perform as a whole – for users, for operations and for organization outcomes. Understanding performance by looking outside the organization helps you direct and influence individual pieces of work for maximum impact.

Creating a service list from the perspective of customers and users is a relatively simple task that can have profound effects on how an organization sees the world. Once that list exists, it will seem odd that it didn't before.

Make services visible

People often misunderstand or aren't in agreement about what a service is. Lou Downe created principles for what makes a good service.[1] Develop a shared view in your organization by (re)defining what a service means. Start with the following definition and adapt it for your organization.

> A service helps someone to do something or to bring about something, where an organization has a desired outcome that it wishes to achieve.

1. A service describes what someone would actually want to do

Start with what people actually want to do in relation to your organization. Not the means, but the end goal. People don't want to have to manage funding or report information. They want to be able to do things like

- drive a car,
- go on holiday,
- get a mortgage,
- get a vaccine,
- open a bank account,
- get a new passport,
- get financial support,
- find a job,
- see a dentist,
- travel to work,
- get an eye test,

- work in a different country,
- get treatment and health care to support the best outcome,
- pay the right tax, or
- have their recycling and rubbish collected.

This doesn't mean that everyone gets to do what the service name implies. A successful service outcome can mean saying no: denying someone access to a firearm, or preventing funding going to a landowner who is polluting a river. But naming our services according to how a user would think of them gives us a way of connecting all the activities involved, including everything that happens before an organization even thinks its service has started. It includes the entire life cycle of 'using' or 'doing' whatever the service provides until it ends.

2. A service has a desired outcome for the organization

Services have a purpose, and that purpose relates to what an organization is there to do. This could be a goal, an intended outcome, or the mission or business model of the organization. The purpose is never just 'revenue', in the same way that public services are not there solely to deliver cost savings. Rather, it's the way in which it is believed an organization will generate profit or fulfil its remit. An example would be the goal to get more people using lower-carbon or electric modes of travel. Or preventing people avoidably losing their eyesight. Or reducing inequalities in wealth.

3. A service includes all the steps between the user, the provider and any other involved actors

A service includes everything that goes on for users and providers, whether that's online, on paper, by phone or by text, face to face, or in any other way. For users it also includes all the bits we wish didn't happen (or don't even know about). It includes how people find out what to do in the first place – sometimes from the wrong sources – and it includes failing to find our service at all. It also includes waiting too long for a decision and then having to chase for answers. And it includes the reasons why someone might then fail to meet the rules of the service, such as forgetting or not being able to renew something in time. If we don't include it, we won't consider how to design to avoid it. A service also includes all the tasks that operational staff need to do, as well as the workarounds that they've had to develop because they haven't been given helpful tools. How well services perform is heavily impacted by our ways of working together, and by the processes and procedures that people carry out to get the job done.

4. A service includes everything involved in delivering it

A service isn't just the parts the user sees or does. And it's never just the 'look and feel'. Services include everything to do with how they are delivered. Organizations sometimes assume that making a better service is about arranging websites, chatbots, kiosks, emails or phone calls. But in reality, the biggest influences on how well services perform are often to do with how an organization functions under the surface. This means the technology, the tools and the systems, the commercial decisions, arrangements and relationships, as well as the people themselves and the culture or values they embody: do organizations believe that customers set out to defraud them, or that most people are trying to be responsible?

*

Use the four prompts above as a guide to make a list of all the services of your organization. Imagine how a customer or user would think of those services or search for them online. Some organizations appear to provide dozens of separate services at first glance, but if you focus on what customers and users really need to do, it's just a handful of services, or even just one.

Figure 1. Make a list of services.

Even if a service has a different name commercially as a brand, or is known by something else publicly, write down services as if they were a sentence that starts with a verb.[2] Something like 'move goods across the border' is considerably clearer and more reflective of the whole goal than 'statutory notice G43Z application form for licence to export as a registered business'. Some organizations have a habit of calling everything a service: teams, projects, policies, systems, technologies, tools, processes, data or anything else. Because of this, people will ask you: 'But what about internal services?' This is a reasonable question, but it is not the right one to ask. The entire point is to establish services from the perspective of customers and users outside the organization. To redefine the organization from the outside in, not to carry on seeing it solely through the lens of existing processes and functions.

Distinguish between main and supporting services

If you end up with a very long list of services, separate them into more manageable and useful categories.

1. Main services.
2. Supporting services.
3. Information and tools that route people to services.

1. Main services

These are core to the purpose of the organization or area of policy. They're the services that make a major difference in people's lives or to the livelihood of businesses. In the public sector they reflect important areas of policy or institutional remit, as well as what's important to citizens, customers and users. Examples include becoming a citizen, learning to drive, getting a passport, getting a mortgage, starting a business or getting a divorce. It's main services such as these that the rest of the advice in this book targets. They are the most important, and they also carry the greatest cost and opportunity.

2. Supporting services

These are also services that help users with a transaction, but they usually only exist because of the way the main services operate. When designed well, they can become an integral part of the main service, so that they're not separate at all, but in many cases they support tasks that happen at a very different point in time or by different users. Examples of supporting services are when you submit information about a change in circumstances, when your driving licence is checked, when a decision is appealed, when performance is reported or when you request a replacement document. These services are not so valuable in their own right, but they can perform important administrative tasks in and around the main services.

These services are smaller. This can make them good candidates for having digitized parts or for creating examples of different ways of working. This won't translate into such meaningful change for the rest of the organization, however.

3. Other information and tools

It's not enough to just make services available. People have to know they exist, be able to find them, understand them and choose between them. This category therefore includes all the content, guidance, advice and interactive tools that can help people figure out what to do to find the right service in the first place, or to connect services together to try to hide complexity.

These are usually not whole services in their own right. More often it involves guidance that helps people work out what to do and where to go, or connects or blends services by offering advice. Examples in this category include information about how much you can borrow, what your mortgage repayments will be, what happens when you turn 18, what to do if you lose your job, or a guide to everything you need to do to start a business.

These things don't necessarily belong in a service list, but it's worth knowing about this category, as guidance and tools serve a valuable purpose in helping people successfully do the right thing. They are good candidates for creating and improving content, and for simplifying rules to make it easier for people to understand and do the right thing – all of which is likely to have an impact on operational efficiency.

The New Zealand government has consolidated information that helps people 'find the right services for you and your child'.[3] NatWest bank offers guidance to first-time buyers on all the steps involved in buying a home, not just help with applying for a mortgage.[4] The UK government design system offers a 'step-by-step' design to help connect all the different tasks across a service.[5]

Divide services into categories with the same purpose

Many services can be divided into categories with the same purpose. This is one way to identify what's similar across services, even if they're doing quite different things. For example, many public sector services are about doing something that requires state permission. Visas, driving licences, permits, certificates, tickets and passes are all forms of permission.[6]

A few of the most common service types help people to

- start something;
- request or claim something;
- do something with permission;
- stop something;
- move people, things or goods;
- learn something;
- become something;
- get or buy something;
- make an agreement about something;
- store something; or
- gain entry or access to something.

The following can often be classified as 'supporting services':

- paying for something;
- getting a token of permission, identity or qualification;
- registering information or telling government about something
- proving, sharing or checking something; and
- getting help with something.

Services that are related include similar (or even the same) stages to them. Knowing what two or more services have in common can resonate with and help individuals and professions who are seeking to reduce duplication of effort or bring greater consistency across an organization.

Show and define what isn't a service

Don't go too large or too small when defining services. Services are more specific and smaller than 'be safe', 'have a livelihood' or 'the criminal justice system'. That doesn't mean you can't consider how well systems work as a whole. But your definitions need to be actionable by the organization you're working with. They're also bigger than 'complete form V30 as per the regulation'.

Watch out for sentences that start with a verb that describes what an organization wants. This demonstrates that activity is being seen only from the perspective of the organization and what it requires people to do rather than from the perspective of what someone actually needs or wants to do. Go up a level to establish what the user is really trying to achieve as the main service, or recognize it as a supporting service.

Occasionally, what an organization requires people to do is unavoidably prescriptive. The UK government has an 'Apply for a National Insurance number' service to make sure national insurance and tax contributions are recorded against your name. This is required by several public services. But these sorts of services should be the exception and not the rule.

Some services – 'get financial support because of poor health' or 'get funding to take environmental or climate action', for example – are most usefully defined around when a life, business or work situation changes.

Embed the service view of the organization

It's one thing to identify services. It's another to start to use services and their performance to influence 'change and improvement' work across the organization. A good first step is to develop a list of services that can be shared and communicated.

Work with others to refine the service view

Work with others and continue to develop the service list so that it starts to become a shared asset for the organization. In meetings and conversations start talking about all the services the organization provides. This will prompt questions and comments. Challenges are helpful too. They shine a light on the different perspectives of people you'll encounter as you work towards a shared and official view of the organization defined by its services, and this will help you develop a more compelling rationale and story for redefining the organization in this way. Your harshest critic can be incredibly insightful.

Share the list with a few people who have the big picture in mind – people who have the capacity to envision the organization in different ways. It won't be 'right' or comprehensive yet, and that's OK. If you show other people something that isn't right, they'll want to tell you what's wrong, and that's exactly the sort of feedback that's helpful.

The next step is to find the right individuals to work with you to iterate the service list. It is important to involve and work alongside those that are already trying to bring sense and clarity to a complex organization. But it is critical to spend time with the people closest to the services themselves – to build shared recognition and common ground. Keep an early eye on who you are likely to need to win support – or at least acceptance – from if you are going to be able to make more profound changes later. You can even ask outright – something along the lines of:

> Who else needs to see this; or who, if they were fully onboard, do you think would help reassure others or pave the way to keep this consistent view of what we do from the perspective of users? What would make this particularly useful, given what we're all trying to make happen? Is it to make the link with transformation work? Or the technology we're responsible for maintaining? Or mapping costs and volumes to it? Or seeing it in the context of policy or operational decisions?

Some people worry if their own area, team or mental model of the organization isn't reflected in the service view of the organization. It's worth reassuring people about this. I say something like:

> This isn't a list of everything the organization does. It doesn't include important corporate services like finance, procurement and HR, or any of our internal services. It's only the external-facing services that relate to the overall organization remit, purpose or policy. I haven't referred to team names, technology or systems in this because it needs to be written in the way that someone who doesn't know our organization might think about it, or type it into Google, not just what we happen to call it internally. It's not finished either – we'll continue to improve it over time.

There will be alternative views of the organization that are already in use, such as its internal 'business' capabilities or other internal 'architecture' and how it is arranged. These views often depict what the organization does on the inside, but without necessarily connecting this with how well it all works on the outside, or with how changes being made 'under the hood' could improve this or perhaps worsen it. It can be useful to work together on developing a shared view of the relationship between the supporting capabilities, technology and processes and the externally facing services, to start to expose these connections. Or perhaps to explain why the view of what happens behind the scenes is not the same as redefining the organization in terms of its externally facing services.

Publish a list of services

Start with a spreadsheet, a text document or pen and paper. The list should change a lot at first. Many different people will need to be able to view it and feel comfortable they're able to contribute to versions of it. When the frequency of changes drops, or you want to control editing rights, you can make a simple web page or internal prototype. Include details such as

- what the list is and what it isn't, in case someone feels worried that their part isn't there or that it doesn't reflect their mental model;
- who it's for (perhaps that it's for internal reference only);
- the name of the organization(s) or parts of the organization that are involved in the service, or the names of teams or individual leaders if they exist;
- the date it was last updated; and
- who to contact if it's wrong, if something's missing or if anyone has questions.

Some organizations publish their service list publicly.[7] This makes it easier to share internally, with suppliers and even with potential new hires. Other organizations keep a version in shared folders or on their intranet. Suppliers and contractors often don't have access to intranets or secure folders, but they need to be able to see it and use it. You don't want them to repeat the work. Make sure it's accessible to those you want to be able to refer to it. In the interests of showing people the work you are doing,[8] some teams write public blog posts to share their service list.[9]

Protect service names and conventions

It is inevitable that an internal view will creep back into a list of service names over time if that is not carefully guarded against. It can help to establish light governance to protect the naming conventions and to give the right people editing control. One way to do this is to establish ownership of the list with the business or operational owners closest to major groups of services. In addition, give overall naming control to people with professional content or service design skills. Pairing people together like this helps keep the content accurate, and the names simple and clear, while protecting the integrity of this outward-facing view.

Start before you have permission

Once an organization has a practical service view of itself like this, few people will question the need for it. But it won't happen unless you make it so. Have the conversations, make a first pass at a list, and push it forwards. The wider opportunities to use it to align teams and their work will become self-evident.

Summary

① Organizations tend to think they know their customers and users, but they often only view the problems through the lens of their existing products and services.

② Re-establish services from the user's perspective to assess performance as a whole, to reveal hidden problems, as well as to solve known challenges.

③ A service

- describes what someone would actually want to do;
- has a desired outcome for the organization;
- includes all the steps between the user, other actors and providers; and
- includes everything involved in delivering it.

④ Make a list of services and start to embed this outside-in definition of your organization, as part of the scaffolding for driving improvement.

A practical shift in talking about what we do
British Red Cross

British Red Cross is an international humanitarian charity that helps people in the UK and around the world get the help they need in a crisis.[10] It works alongside many other organizations involved in disaster response and recovery, including 'bluelight' services, governments, other voluntary organizations and communities. In a complex landscape such as this, the 'core offer' of an organization can be hard to fix and agree on. British Red Cross took an outside-in approach to address this by building a shared view of its services to people. Examples included 'get emergency cash', 'get urgent help' and 'find missing family after an emergency'. The intention was that defining services in this way kept the focus on outcomes. But it also showed the huge range of services, and it began to reveal gaps in how services were being delivered, as well as the reality of who was affected and involved in them. Jo Straw, the transformation programme manager for British Red Cross, explains:

> Defining our services in this way was a very practical shift in how we talk about what we do – and this helped move decision making forwards.
>
> Our operations and digital transformation teams worked together to build a shared view. We linked the services back to our organizational strategy. Our services need to be a practical delivery route of some of the wider aims. For example, reducing the administrative burden so teams can spend more time on valuable humanitarian work – or enabling many of the other organizations involved in disaster recovery to achieve outcomes. This gave teams focus. It helped us decide how to invest in new skills and roles to better support services and priorities.
>
> It also showed us the opportunity to use the vast insight and experience British Red Cross has in disaster recovery, to take more of a leadership and influencing role among other actors in the system.

Joined-up services as a business model
Boxt

Integrating lots of separate tasks into one cohesive service can be a business opportunity. To replace a boiler in your home, you usually have to pick one from a manufacturer based on their overly complex specifications and then find an installer. You'll hope the boiler will fit where the old one was and that it's right for your house, or you'll find a plumber to ask. And you need to remember to get it regularly serviced, choosing from extended warranties or home care or insurance.

By joining all of this together, Boxt offers a whole 'get and own a boiler' service.[11] You answer questions about your home and send in a few photos. They guide you to the right product to buy while also finding and organizing a registered engineer for installation and repairs, with people available along the way to help and reassure you.

Chapter 2

Define what's in a service from the outside in

This isn't just another way to describe an organization. It's a new way of seeing what that organization is there to do.

Defining services from the outside in does not mean defining the 'user journey' as if it's entirely separate to all the internal systems and processes. Rather, it means starting with what users are trying to do, and including everything that's involved in using or delivering the service: the bits that users see, what operational and frontline teams do and how, support models and processes, all the bits of technology and the data.

By defining what's in a service from the outside in you give the organization a different viewpoint and language to reposition what it does and for whom.

It's valuable for other practical reasons too. Without a consistent view, every team, project, portfolio and programme develops its own way to describe what it's doing and why. Like the parable of the blind men and the elephant, people only know their part of the service, rather than the whole thing and how their part relates to it. Having many different views, plans and roadmaps makes it difficult for an organization to understand the overall picture or progress, or to manage how coherent or possible it all is. Are we doing the right things in the right ways for the outcomes we seek? Are we making use of the right skill sets to do this?

With the tools to define service stages, and to agree the language and have a shared understanding of what success looks like, this chapter helps you to bring connection and direction to what can otherwise be separate and chaotic. And in a way that will resonate with everyone.

Draw the stages, not the process

Services have many different parts. Service stages represent something important that needs to happen – something that dictates what happens next. Each stage has a desired outcome: what happens if that part of the service works really well. A good test is whether you can state the ideal result objectively, with an idea for how to recognize success. This starts to form the top level of an organizing framework.

Get permission to do something

| Find out | Choose & act | Decide | Issue & fulfil | Use & comply | Enforce | Change or renew | Get help |

Get financial support for something

| Identify the need | Choose | Claim or apply | Decide or agree | Pay | Take action | Verify or report | Change |

Request or set something up

| Discover | Apply | Decide | Order & set up | Use | Pay | Change/ upgrade | Renew/ leave | Get help |

Figure 2. Service stages.

Use a verb and keep the description short, so that it's abstract. The goal is to identify the stages that will endure, no matter what changes about how it works or how it's supported operationally. These are the backbone of *what a service does*.

This is not about setting out processes people are meant to follow, or steps they have to complete themselves. A process only describes how something happens to work today, which could be due to historic decisions or constraints that no longer exist.

What's more valuable is to establish a consistent, *outside-in* view. The stages should do just as well for mapping what we know about customers and users as they do for understanding the technology or data that underpins whole services.

The examples I've included here blend together the steps for customers and users with how a service is operated and delivered. The emphasis is usually on one or the other at different times, so combining them makes it widely useful whether you need the whole picture or just need to analyse one aspect. If you find this confuses people, underneath the high-level stages you can add the steps for external users and steps to represent what happens behind the scenes.

Most services start with someone realizing the need to do something, understanding there's a service for it, and then actually finding that service. This takes place before most organizations think their services start. We can think of this as a 'find out' or 'identify the need' stage.

Of course, services aren't linear. Real life is messy. There are loops, backtracking and missed stages. There are stages like 'get help' that need to be there the whole time. And there are a whole lot of mini steps within. These are imperfect models designed to be good enough to help you organize.

Defining the service stages brings clarity through its abstraction. But what's unique is the view it provides of customers and users alongside the changes being made under the hood. It's a thinking tool as well as an organizing tool to help everyone bring their best ideas about how it can all work better, whether they're a technologist, an operational or policy lead, a designer, or a fraud or compliance specialist.

If the service doesn't exist yet, guess the likely stages and use them as a way to organize the work to be done, to identify the questions that need to be answered and what you need to learn.

Put these stages as headings at the top of diagrams. Doing this gives a consistent framework, making it easier to connect everything: technology, data, teams, projects, performance indicators or insight from user research. As long as you brought others along with you during the process for developing the stages, they should provide a collective view of a service that's encompassing enough that everyone can see where their work fits.

When you need to know what happens outside an individual service, a broader 'system' or 'lived experience' view can also provide context and understanding: a depiction of what life is like for people who use services, perhaps, or the life cycle of a broader activity that the service fits into; or another abstraction that brings sense and order to what can feel from the outside like disparate pieces of work. Examples of this approach would be

- a map of the whole criminal justice system,[1]
- the whole process of buying or selling a house,
- mapping major life events and organizing services and guidance around them,[2]
- the life of a farmer and what's involved in the annual farming cycle, and
- the wider context for why someone may need poverty support or a food stamps system.[3]

Although beware spending what can feel like endless amounts of time depicting very complex systems across organizations without being able to improve or change them.

Change the language to ingrain services

For organizations that are modernizing or transforming, there's a tendency to obsess about IT and technology, rather than the culture, practices and processes that are often the bigger prize.

Technology is radically changing entire industries and public domains. Many organizations are in dire need of modern technology and processes, but they are enablers rather than the point. Choosing, improving or overhauling technology should be done in a way that moves services towards what good looks like.

One large organization spent many months mapping their internal 'business capabilities' in a consistent way. Once they'd done so, it was presumed that teams and leaders would use capability mapping as a tool to direct work. But the mapping alone didn't say anything about the 'performance' of these capabilities: whether they were good, bad or improving. It described what existed, but this didn't help leaders to connect it to their own goals or financial drivers. It was only when a 'performance framework' was developed that anchored what was happening externally for the services these capabilities supported that it became a genuinely useful, shared tool for leaders and teams alike.

Figure 3. A shared language for different parts of a service.

Develop a shared language for all the different parts of your service that places the external-facing elements at the top. Everything below them enables (or hinders) how well they work. It's an ontology that describes what services are made of – but it also sets out the right relationships between the component parts. Unlike other frameworks, it's all-encompassing, so there's room to include the messy, real world of humans using services in its very definition.

In the pages that follow I set out an example that you can adapt to develop a shared language that works for your organization.

Services

What external customers and users are trying to do or achieve, where there's an outcome for the provider that relates to their core purpose.

Activities or tasks

All the activities undertaken by users, as well as everything that happens internally. For users it includes the reality of what happens, such as 'waiting', 'chasing up to see what's happened' and 'feeling worried'. Internally it's everything involved in the service: 'verifying identity', 'checking eligibility' and 'communicating a decision', for example.

Capabilities

This is everything that's needed to enable whole services and any supporting products and transactions – a way to support appointment booking, invoicing or payments, for example. This might include people, teams, processes or ways of working, as well as the underlying technology, data or physical infrastructure needed to support services.

Technology

Here we are talking about the technology, IT and systems involved in services that form their supporting capabilities. This

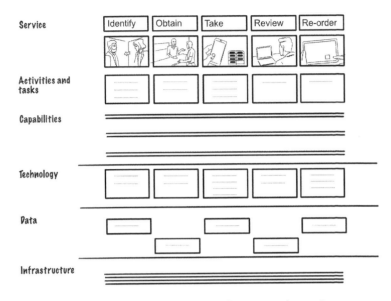

Figure 4. A template for an outside-in map of a service.

includes the internal systems and tools that we give to internal users to operate the service, the technology that performs tasks on people's behalf, the technology that is exposed to external users, and the technology that enables teams to build or develop parts of services faster.*

---

* Some organizations would identify products as a category. Note that 'product' means different things to different people in different sectors, which makes them infamously hard to define. A product can be software that is used to do something and that is being actively developed and improved. Products can be externally facing or internally facing: an online billing system or a mobile app, for example. They can be physical objects that are manufactured, such as a mobile phone, or 'sellable' packages, such as a mobile phone insurance policy. A mobile phone, an online billing system, an app and an insurance policy could make up some of the parts of an end-to-end service. Whether 'products' is useful as a concept to describe what a service is made from varies between organizations, teams and sectors, so I don't separate it out as its own category here.

Data

This refers to the data that's used, created, stored or changed by services. It can include the data itself, as well as standards for how it's formatted, handled and used. It also includes legal and ethical requirements for personal data, as well as details about where or how it's stored or hosted.

Infrastructure

The infrastructure is the facilities that underpin service provision, from the physical space needed, to the equipment that will be used, to Wi-Fi or cloud hosting arrangements.

*

Categories and relationships like those above have helped many organizations and teams map out and develop consistent views about how a service works or how it could work in future. They help to link views of underlying capabilities and technology to what good looks like for each stage of a service, and they make clear the relationships between the pieces of work we do internally and how they affect users, operations and outcomes. Sarah Drummond developed an overarching model of 'full stack service design' that reflects the parts I've listed here, and includes how culture and intent influence the success of services (which this book looks at in later chapters).[4]

Create a consistent framework to describe services

Establishing service stages and a shared language provides an overarching framework that has provided many organizations with a practical way to

- demonstrate how a service works today, or how it could work radically differently in future;

- show what customers and users are actually doing or failing to do at each stage and what impact this has;
- map out supporting capabilities, including the actual technology, tools, data and infrastructure – or what's needed; and
- communicate likely transition states during major change – who is doing what, what is changing, what is happening now and the intention in twelve months' time, say.

To make a first sketch of what the stages are, we can use our expert and domain knowledge about what happens, or what we think should happen. But to know what good looks like, and to understand the issues at hand, we have to observe what actually happens in real life with real people.

Escape the curse of knowledge by observing what actually happens

Many organizations only view the problems users face through their feedback channels about existing processes: surveys, contact centres or complaints. It's not possible to know everything that's going on outside when you're deep inside.

The best way to get to know customers and users is to see for yourself what actually happens: to follow a handful of people from before the start until after the finish of an important service; or to talk to them immediately after each step, before they've forgotten how it went.

The goal is to find out

- what happens and why;
- what's easy and what's difficult; and
- what works or doesn't work, for whom, and in which situations.

Consider whatever it is that happens before and after the part you're interested in. For example, how did someone even come to know what to do? This kind of user research is broad. Some of what you learn will definitely fall outside the scope of any single organization, programme or team. If it does, it's a sign you're doing it right: you want a human in a real situation to be the focus, not an existing process or product.

Aim to learn from eight to twelve customers and users to start with. Add more if you get wildly different stories. You won't pick up on everything, but it will give you first-hand experience of the main issues in a way that's hard to ignore.

What happens behind the scenes

Follow what happens operationally inside the organization to process a case or application or to progress a situation. I've often sat with the people making an application and then walked alongside huge bundles of paper as the received application is taken on a trolley from the mailroom, where it's tagged and scanned, to the desk of someone triaging incoming cases, before finally arriving with a caseworker. I've then observed someone reading the letter that tells them about a decision several times, but still not really understanding if it's a yes or a no.

User research like this isn't the only way to know anything. It would take a very long time and be very expensive to learn all we need to know about services by studying individual cases. People in operations and contact centres already understand a great deal of what does and doesn't work, but it's still incredibly valuable for people to see and feel it for themselves. That said, be aware that it's deeply irritating when observers proudly report back insights they've gleaned first hand as though they're the only one to know them – especially for the operational staff who have spent the last five years knowing the problems without having the means to change them.

As well as understanding what's hard about each step, we're also looking to understand at a high level what's actually going on and why. Build on and verify what was learned from your research by asking internal experts to give their feedback on what you've seen and to add their experience to it. These experts will have rare levels of knowledge, so knowing how to extract the most useful parts is important.[5] If they talk about processes, ask them why they do it this way and not that way. If they speak in terms of IT systems, find out about the activities they support and the typical problems that are encountered. If they mention ideas and solutions, ask what's useful and what isn't useful, and under which conditions; ask what's most important too. The experts can often provide context for the problems that users face – such as tasks that might have a very valid reason for existing even if users struggle with them. The key to this is not what *could* go wrong, but what *does* go wrong, and how often, because if it's predictable, we can do something about it.

Work with a specialist user researcher

It's the job of a professional user researcher to help teams learn about users and services.[6] The advice in this section isn't meant to replace the many years of study and practice it takes to do this well, while avoiding the pitfalls and navigating the ethical and data protection issues. Rather, the goal is to reinforce the importance of having professional researchers in service organizations to help teams know about their users. There are superb resources and guides for how to hire the right people and carry out good user research,[7] but this area is unfortunately far beyond the scope of this book.

Understand what's hard about operating a service

What's helpful for front-line staff and operations is having everyone else care just as much as they do about how it can feel safer, more controlled and more predictable to deliver services. It's part of working as a whole, to create the tools and change the conditions to make it easier to operate well.

It's important for everyone to understand the peaks and troughs of demand, as well as the operational issues for major services. If services follow seasonal cycles, a simple traffic-light system is one way to communicate to many others what the difficult and busiest time periods are and why.

Steer conversations towards what's hard operationally for a service, rather than what's hard from a management perspective. For example, people might feel stressed more often during very busy months, making it hard to manage shifts. But shift management is a management issue, not a service issue. Understanding what makes those months busy and stressful is more important for knowing what to change, to better manage and control volumes.

It's also useful to know the ebb and flow of demand across a service for other reasons:

- Any change to existing services, or to parts of them, or the creation of a new service will need to be handled in line with what currently makes everyone busy at certain times of the year or in certain situations.
- Knowing about current demand and bottlenecks will help people see how to solve them.
- If we give people poorly designed tools, or we support operations badly in other ways, we shouldn't be surprised by bottlenecks. People can rightly be resistant if they've had experiences of being blamed for delays that resulted from changes being made that they weren't involved in or where they weren't listened to. The least we can all do is start to properly understand the full picture and these relationships and experiences.

Map out what happens across the operational cycle or end-to-end service with colleagues as well as looking at the impact that it has. People begin to hear each other. Awareness will start to build. A good sign of the culture of separation changing is when everyone else mentions the drawbacks of particular ideas, deadlines or plans because of risks to operational deliverability.

Say what good looks like

When a service doesn't work well for users, it's usually hard to operate – and vice versa. For each of a service's stages, say what has to happen before the next stage can be reached. Write a short, factual statement about the ideal consequence of that stage. It's sometimes a matter of stating the opposite of the problems you observed or heard from users. Some common examples of what good looks like for different stages would be

- users knowing what to do;
- users choosing the right option for their situation;
- having the right data to make a decision that's right first time;
- users being confident they've done the right thing or that the right thing is now happening;
- a decision being made and communicated, and users understanding it;
- a token of permission or the right payment being issued securely to the right person;
- being able to accurately tell who has permission to do something and who hasn't.

By establishing what good looks like in this way, you are combining user and operational needs. This gives critical context to all the arrangements, technology, tools, data and processes that support the service.

Summary

① The stages in a service describe what happens for customers as well as internal operations.

② Carry out user research to find out what good looks like for each stage, for users and for operations.

③ Develop a shared language for supporting capabilities to help people with different backgrounds work together.

④ Service stages and a shared language give a consistent way to develop service views that connect what happens for users with what goes on internally.

⑤ State what good looks like for each stage in a service to guide direction for all supporting capabilities and activity.

Creating a service view of the whole organization
HM Passport Office, UK

HM Passport Office is the issuer of UK passports and is responsible for civil registration services in England and Wales through the General Register Office.

Colin Foley is the head of business and service design and describes how creating a view of the whole passport service has helped to align the work of many different functions.[8]

> As an organization we're very customer facing. That focus has always been integral to our culture. If the passport service doesn't work well, our customers feel it, and our customer support staff and examiners see it immediately in what comes back to them. But we didn't all have the same sense of the end to end. Policy had a view but not necessarily of the customer's perspective. Case management only saw their bit, customer support was separate, there were lots of suppliers and contractual arrangements involved and the people who managed suppliers were separate to the casework teams. Agile delivery teams working

on individual parts of the service couldn't always see how their work fitted in. We'd make decisions or solve problems for one part without being able to see the impact or the coherence across the whole.

We created a viewpoint of the service that looked end to end across all the stages, including the customer-facing parts, all the things we do behind the scenes and which teams or suppliers were involved. We blended this with the decisions we were making at each step of the service – and on what basis we were making those decisions. This formed a map of the whole service, as well as a framework that set out what we needed and what good looked like, with metrics and other indicators to tell us how efficient and effective the service was.

The service map provided a useful view that worked well for our operational managers, but also the decision makers, the policy folks and our agile teams – who could show which part of the service they were working on. It gave us the tools, views and metrics that were useful when issues came up. When people were making decisions, they could see it all more holistically: 'You're using these teams or these suppliers in these stages', 'This is what you're trying to get from it', 'This is how you'll see what works and what doesn't'. People started to see naturally what they hadn't seen before; not just the part where we receive someone's application, but the whole thing.

The organization was already investing in digital transformation. We started mapping the transformation activity to the service map. But it was clear that a service map like this should be something you always use when you're a service provider, with or without a transformation, because it puts the focus on users and on operational decision makers. It's not just about digital; it helps you with business as usual, and it works for policy, operations, strategy, digital teams and leadership. The service map and framework sparked people's interest. We had new senior leaders joining, and it also gave them the tools to see the whole picture.

Using common patterns as the building blocks of services
BT Group plc

BT Group plc is one of the world's leading communications services companies, operating the BT, EE and Plusnet brands.

Jeanette Clement is the head of service design and user research for BT Group plc. She shares how they use commonality across services to help large numbers of teams and disciplines collaborate to improve the experience for customers as well as internal users.[9]

> Service patterns have helped us unpick some of the complexity of user journeys and our services at BT, to help us improve efficiency in what we design and develop.
>
> A pattern is a step that's similar or repeated across different services. For BT's services, these could be 'book something', 'compare and choose', 'check usage' and 'pay'. It includes the things a user interacts with, and all of the things that make it happen behind the scenes.
>
> BT is a very large organization. We have many teams all designing very similar things in parallel, which they may not be aware of. But the result is duplicated effort in design, development, architecture and support. We've identified over 40 of these service patterns so that we can:
>
> - Create consistent experiences between different journeys to help build familiarity and confidence.
> - Bring teams closer together to align and share knowledge.
> - Provide a starting point for designing steps in new journeys based on what we know works or doesn't.
> - Operate more efficiently with building blocks that are repeatable, scalable and re-usable for a service. Such as creating ways for different bits of technology to 'talk' to each other (e.g. APIs), improving data availability or

standards, building new technology or changing legal arrangements.

We are also collaborating with colleagues across BT to consider how reflecting service patterns in our organizational structure and engineering processes can help us to be more efficient.

Seeing patterns across services
The Department for Levelling Up, Housing and Communities, UK

The Department for Levelling Up, Housing and Communities (DLUHC) in the UK provides many different forms of funding to local institutions, e.g. the Levelling Up fund, the UK Community Renewal fund and the Towns fund. These funds are intended to deliver different outcomes, but the users are often the same people, teams, communities or organizations.

Funding services follow a similar pattern of stages between users and providers: users finding out about funds and applying, followed by a decision, an agreement or award and set up of funding, and then delivery, reporting and learning.

DLUHC digital teams are working on a project to deliver regeneration funds in a more efficient and user-friendly way using modern digital approaches. But the team has an eye on the possibility of then reusing this infrastructure and common service patterns in other areas. One option is that rather than, say, seven funding teams all developing separate online forms and ways to store data, it might make sense to develop common capabilities that can support different types of funding, with the benefit of applying appropriate standards for the handling of data or inclusive design. You could imagine moving towards a 'single' funding service, that routes users to the right type of funding, depending on their situation or the intended outcome, supported by a smaller set of modern capabilities that can be well looked after, that are then safer and more secure to operate.

But one of the reasons for having different funds is that they have different outcomes. A fund could be to plant trees, or build a new junction off a motorway, or develop housing. These might use entirely different data, even if it's from the same users. The considerable cost and effort of attempting to develop a single design, data store, piece of technology, or whole service when it varies so much (and when the priorities of the organization change) might not be worth it.

Alice Whitehead, service owner for funding at DLUHC, explains:[10]

> The more you look at services and technology in abstract, the more similar it can all appear. But services that sound similar at a distance can have very different outcomes and require quite different handling. It needs a deeper dive to understand the reality, the actual opportunity and the risks. What we have done is to embed an outwards view that's user focused, and blend that with the outcomes we're trying to achieve across the organization. Service steps and service patterns are an organizing framework that's recognizable and useful to the organization. To create a good service you need more than just a view of the internal workings in abstract. For us that also means reminding people that while we take time to decide about funding applications, users are there waiting, thinking, chasing, and it can be nerve wracking. We share real human stories and evidence of the impact, to bring reality to abstraction.

Organizations and specialists working together to improve a service
Getting support as a family
When different organizations are involved, mapping out the whole service together can help identify where or how to join things up. 'Getting support as a family in a difficult situation' isn't a linear transactional service, and it isn't provided by just one

organization.[11] Depending on what's needed, a family could be referred by a school to a local authority's early help team. It might involve the local educational psychology service, a children's centre and support groups, as well as individual specialists such as family workers or domestic abuse specialists. These teams come together to focus on what the family needs. Building a shared view of what's available and how to improve it by working with other specialists can have greater impact at scale. This includes funders, leadership, designers, technologists and data specialists, in addition to service workers and family specialists.

Chapter 3

Reveal how services perform in the real world

How well a service performs means how well it works for people, how well everything involved in delivering it works, and what the outcomes are.

Now that we know what our services are and have a consistent way of showing what they're made of, let's look at how well they work for users and operations, and with what outcomes.

Organizations will think they already measure the important things – because they have a reporting function, data analysts and a business planning process. But this kind of reporting is often about the performance of separate functions, or the progress of disjointed bits of delivery. Because it's all separate, there's no way for leadership to tell if services are good or bad, or if they're achieving outcomes or performing better as a result of investment.

Teams have different ways of looking at the individual parts. They might be

- reviewing the ease, speed or safety with which we can deliver changes to live services, change capabilities or respond to new priorities;

- looking through an operational lens, including throughput, bottlenecks, wait times, issue resolution, quality of response or outcome, handling time or cost;
- taking a technology perspective, assessing availability, speed, security issues and costs;
- evaluating the customer's or user's experience and success rate;
- looking at the level of duplicated effort, the time wasted, the avoidable contact, or other service 'failure' and efficiency improvements;
- assessing acquisition and retention rates, average revenue or cost per user, overall value and support costs;
- assessing how risky, transparent or auditable accounting or compliance processes are.

The truth is, these are all sides of the same coin. Each point describes one aspect of service performance, but not the whole.

Don't spend time trying to convince people that one way of looking at performance is better than another. If a service doesn't work well for users, it will be harder to support, costly to operate and will fail to achieve its purpose. Invest time instead in collectively agreeing performance measures that bring the important perspectives together.

Define the job of a service and its outcomes

A service exists to do a job. In public services there's usually a broader intention that government policy seeks to address. To know if it's working, then, we need to understand the intent, what the service is there to do, and what a good outcome looks like.

The job of social security services isn't necessarily to pay money to everyone, but it might be to make the right payment to an eligible user. Governments can change who is eligible and the level or form of support to better achieve policy intent at any given time, but that doesn't necessarily change what constitutes a successful service outcome.

In terms of good outcomes for users, a service can't promise money, but a good service will make the right payments to the right people, without avoidable administrative burden, while being transparent and consistent with decisions. Look at the proportion of service transactions that result in successful and eligible payments to users. Understanding all the ways in which that doesn't happen will give you the means to bring that ratio as close to 1:1 as possible.

Here are a couple of examples.

Policy intent: support people who are unable to work.
Service: get support because of low or no income.
Service outcome: a successful and eligible payment of the right benefits.

Policy intent: protect the public from the spread of disease.
Service: get financial support to stay at home during a pandemic.
Service outcome: a successful and eligible payment in the right time frame (i.e. now).

Every team should be able to say what the outcome is for the service they work on. And they should want to find out or estimate how often a service results in this outcome, and about how often it does not – and why.

Service outcomes are just one way to know more about whether a service delivers policy intent and meets expectations well enough. You'll also want to measure longer-term outcomes and evaluate the extent to which a service delivers the wider intention.

Set indicators for what good looks like

You can use metrics to represent what good looks like as a whole. These include

- how well a service is achieving the intent behind it;
- how often the right service outcome is achieved;
- how well users (and potential users) are supported in what they need or with what they need to do; and
- the time, effort, risk, issues, errors, avoidable burden and cost involved for everyone – users and operations.

These four points are the foundation for understanding good and bad service performance, while being able to run services safely, responsibly and equitably. Only separate out user experience metrics, operational efficiency or delivery metrics when you need to see or learn something specific at that level.

Flip pain points into what we'd see if it worked well

As described in chapter 2, a good way to know how well a service is working is to spend time with people as they try to do whatever it is that they need to do with it. We looked before at how to turn these observations into statements about what good looks like for each step of a service. This chapter translates these qualities into numbers that indicate performance.

The most relevant insight to translate is often the data that describes why a service goes wrong. This is because that is easier to spot and because what goes wrong usually shows us what needs to happen for it to go right. And if we can see that it already happens, it's predictable. Which in turn means we can do something about it. What goes wrong could include

- why people do the wrong thing,
- why they fail to do the right thing,

- why they aren't clear about what to do or what is happening, and
- why we spend lots of additional time fixing problems.

Flip what doesn't work (the pain points, or 'negative' user needs) into what we would see instead if things worked really well.

Imagine for a particular service that user research, operations and contact centre feedback all confirm that

- people are scared of choosing the wrong option because they find it ambiguous or complicated, and the impact of getting it wrong is so severe;
- people choose the wrong option because they can't easily apply the criteria to their own specific situation; and
- people feel worried about whether the right thing is happening after they've submitted an application, and they want to talk to someone to reassure them.

This kind of insight is often the key to understanding patterns and bottlenecks in operations. When we don't help users successfully do what they need to do, it shows up as additional work in our operations. When people aren't confident, the contact centre will handle more contact. When people apply for the wrong thing, the operational team will be busy with extra work and back-and-forth with users. It's what John Seddon (occupational psychologist, author and managing director of Vanguard) calls 'avoidable contact' and 'service failure'. That's because, theoretically, it only happens when the service doesn't work well for the people who need it.[1]

If there was no service failure, the opposite would need to be true. So, for example, that might be because

- people feel confident that they've done it right,
- they choose the right options, and
- they're confident that the right thing is now happening.

To know more about this, we could try one of the following.

- We could ask samples of people to score how confident they feel that they've made the right choice, using a Likert scale (e.g. 1–5, where 1 is 'not at all confident' and 5 is 'very confident'). We could take a view that by increasing the proportion of participants who score 4 or 5, that would be a good indication that we're making the service clearer and simpler. We could test this with a sample of people on a continuous basis or before and after improvement work.
- We could record operational data to see the proportion of applications where people choose the right option for a situation. We would also compare whether those who felt confident went on to make the right choice, since it's equally problematic if people are confidently making the wrong choices.
- We could categorize inbound contact to find out what proportion of people who apply then ask about what is happening or when, or check that they did the right thing.

Much of the value of user research is in bringing qualitative insight to decision making, in order to understand why things don't work and what the opportunities are. But it's entirely possible to count qualitative data, translating a quality into a quantity: *the extent* to which people are confused, or *what proportion* of people get lost, or feel so scared that they don't take action.

Measuring satisfaction or delight isn't always useful
Someone might feel satisfied if something goes well or goes the way they want it to, but measuring satisfaction doesn't by itself tell you what needs to change. For example, some people will feel satisfied by

- a problem being resolved quickly,
- an issue being solved right the first time,

- getting a refund or
- feeling validated or properly listened to.

Some people won't think anything at all about a service if it works seamlessly. In some cases, trying to make someone love a service is wasted effort, when simply not having to think about it is the ideal.

Research indicates that people are most often delighted when their initial expectations are dismal[2] or when they were anxious in the first place. This sets the stage for a decent design or effortless resolution to blow them away. It's a common pattern: users have an anxiety-causing problem; they get it easily resolved; then they feel delighted. That's good for us because it means we can find out what these situations are, and anticipate and track them for our services. It's a very different approach from conjuring up unusual features or introducing faddy technology to try to 'delight'.

Of course, different people will be satisfied by different results in different situations. So understand what leads to 'satisfaction' for a particular type of service or segment of users, and then measure that instead.

The concept of customer satisfaction doesn't always sit comfortably in public services. There are services we don't want to have to use, like paying a parking penalty or appealing a court decision. Being shocked by a larger than expected tax bill will not feel satisfying. For this kind of service it can be more practical to assess people's confidence instead: confidence as a user that I'm doing the right thing; confidence that the right thing is now happening.

Some services 'do' things to people. When something is happening that someone doesn't want to happen, the least that might be hoped for is that people will be treated fairly and with respect. We can learn more about this by talking to people – to those involved, to family, friends, carers or representatives – and asking people to self-report their experiences.

How to avoid optimizing what doesn't need to exist

Efficiency is about the time, cost or effort involved in achieving what we need to. Even with very constrained budgets, efficiency is secondary to effectiveness. One well-known problem is spending too much time optimizing processes that wouldn't need to exist if we rethought how parts of a service worked or joined them up, or modelled the risks of something not happening at all.

Look at what happens behind the scenes when a service doesn't work for users. There's usually additional work and contact that might have been avoided, leaving more time to anticipate and focus on what would better support users.

A good way to do this is by comparing what actually happens with what would happen if the service worked perfectly.

Imagine we have a service about making a decision on someone's entitlement to do something: to get a passport for the first time, for example, or to work in the US, get a mortgage or enter a country. We know it takes time to process each decision operationally. That's because we might not receive the data we need, the supporting evidence isn't right, or we have to ask applicants to clarify or send further details. Meanwhile they wait or they call us. Perhaps it takes a lot of effort to figure out their situation to be able to help them.

You could summarize this by measuring the proportion of applications that result in a decision that's right the first time. If the proportion is high, it would suggest that the right people are applying in the first place, and that operations get the right data or use good data to make a robust decision. This would make it less likely that decisions would subsequently be overturned by an assurance or appeals process. There should be a resulting impact on how confident people feel, and on the cost to serve, as a result of better-quality and faster decisions.

Put indicators like this at the heart of service performance and improvement. These are about effectiveness, quality and value. They get to the purpose of the service. And they also drive greater efficiency.

Turn what good looks like into a framework

Having identified stronger indicators for service performance, you can build them up for all stages in a service to develop a coherent picture of what's going on for users, operations and outcomes. Or, at the very least, to set out what the ideal result is for each stage, as well as overall.

If the service is simple and small, what good looks like can feel obvious to the small number of people who work on it. It's when a service has dozens of teams and pieces of work under-way that a framework like this is valuable to help inform work at scale.

In many organizations services aren't seen as a whole, which makes it difficult to get performance data. But the very act of setting out what you're aiming to improve puts you in a much stronger position to assess what's needed, whether you have the numbers or not.

Set measurable goals that help teams work together
When complex services have many different teams and capa-bilities supporting them, a single measurable goal brings clar-ity. For important parts of a service, a single measurable goal brings clarity. For example, for a decision about entitlement to something, a single goal could be: 'get the data right first time to make a robust decision on eligibility'. This focus can help every-one to bring their best thinking on how to achieve it, or work towards it over time.

It also makes it simpler to develop and evaluate business cases or funding requests (because folks know what they're ulti-mately trying to change or improve) and to say no to requests that aren't linked to valuable problems.

Show the ideal service demand funnel
Demand is one term used to describe the volume of people, work or 'need' moving across a service. Many services have an ideal pattern of 'demand', in theory. This is similar to a *conversion funnel*, which retailers think about to optimize the proportion of people who actually go ahead and buy something.

For some services, the ideal pattern of demand is one where users who weren't going to be eligible for something leave the service at the earliest possible point, before too much time is spent on either side.

Thinking of a service in terms of a pattern of demand can help identify or measure access and inclusion or progress issues. Ask questions such as:

1. How many people could or should be using this service? What's the size of the audience or market?

2. How many potential users are aware that they can or should be using the service? Who isn't aware? Is there an awareness problem?

Figure 5. Service demand.

3. How many potential users are doing something about it? Is there an activation problem?

4. How many potential users find their way to the service? Is there a discovery or routing problem?

5. What kinds of user (and in what situations) are not finding or using the service who should or could be?

How to measure and evaluate a service

Author and management consultant Peter Drucker shared the idea that efficiency is about doing things right, and effectiveness is about doing the right things.[3] This is a solid basis for defining whole-service performance. The service organization consultant Matti Keltanen created the following set of common measures of service effectiveness and efficiency that you can use and adapt for your own services.

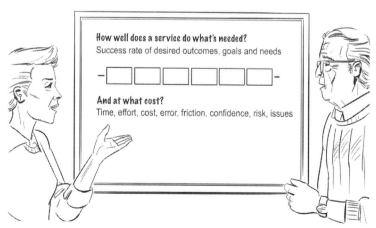

Figure 6. Service measurement model.

Service effectiveness
These are indicators for whether a service does the 'right things'.

- How often does a service transaction result in a successful outcome. For example, the percentage of eligible applications or claims for support that result in the right payment, to the right person or place, in the right time frame.
- How often does a stage in a service result in a successful outcome. For example, the percentage of applications that included the data needed, that were accurate, and that were therefore able to be processed without needing to check, clarify or contact the customer.
- Does the service do what users need to do and is anyone excluded? How does it cause different groups of people to behave or to feel when they use the service?
- To what extent does it deliver the intention of the policy (for public sector services)?
- To what extent it delivers other goals of the organization

Service efficiency
These are indicators of whether a service does these things 'right'. By that we mean minimizing the time, effort or cost involved, and the errors, friction and rework that takes place. In particular, what proportion of this is avoidable or undesirable, in theory at least? For everyone and everything involved: external users, internal users and supporting capabilities. Indicators of service efficiency might include the following.

- Time taken to complete tasks.
- Cumulative time taken overall and between stages.
- Cost and effort.
- Error rates.
- Friction, which might include a 'lostness score'[4] (the number of additional steps that ended up being taken, beyond what

was strictly necessary), the number of steps or tasks, the cognitive load, the inconvenience, and circular loops.

- Avoidable time or effort: retyping, rework, multiple contacts, avoidable contact.

Use these prompts to identify indicators that could tell you how well services are working now, and if they're improving, staying neutral or getting worse.

It's a model – so it's not perfect. You'll need to adjust it according to what makes sense for the particular people, communities, services and systems you're working with. For example, how long it takes someone to do something isn't necessarily important: getting it right or feeling taken care of might matter more. What causes unfair, harmful, systemic and lasting effects for people will vary depending on past experiences, race, financial difficulty, or being part of an unsupportive society or in an unhelpful location, among many factors. What's good for a service that supports the fostering and adoption of children will be vastly different from what's good for a transactional service such as taking the stress out of going from A to B in a taxi.

You don't need to do this for every service or to use every point listed here: just do enough of what's important to demonstrate how to create an enduring, practical view of performance that can help to shape and direct improvement work.

Use with care
I've described a transactional model of service performance here that applies equally well to services or systems with stages. But it's based on the assumption that there's an individual human, customer, user or case moving through it. Of course, not all systems or services work this way. It's a mechanistic view. It doesn't address fundamental themes of equity or the ethics of a service. It doesn't directly capture the overall effect of the service on communities, society, the climate or the environment.

It is not the only way to examine and improve a service and its impacts and biases. But it does start to provide an important view that's often missing from large organizations. And we also still need to be looking at the broader impact as well as the ways in which services will be biased towards certain groups of users over others.

Understanding policy intent and outcomes doesn't reduce the chance that the intent might be harmful, badly thought through, or in conflict with another policy. The service might have no impact at all and yet you end up measuring it anyway. Applying the ideas in this section won't make a service perfect, but doing so is a good way of bringing together all the different views into a tool that supports better decision making.

Influence with the data you don't yet have

Figure out what you want to know first – worry about getting the numbers later. How certain or uncertain you already are will dictate how worthwhile it is spending time getting more exact information.[5]

You often won't need this kind of performance data continuously, or in real time, so it can be worth the one-off effort to dig it up or calculate it approximately, with some help from operational, performance analysis or economist colleagues.

Not having an exact number is not the same as knowing nothing at all. People who work on a service will generally already know when and where it's bad. Users drop out too early. Ineligible applications make it too far along the process. It takes ages to sort things out when something goes wrong. You can always know something about a number by

- figuring out what it is that you would want to know and determining it subjectively, i.e. making an educated guess;
- looking at small sample sizes, which will tell you much more than failing to look at them; and

- substituting some other data because it is representative enough, i.e. using a proxy.

Don't wait to be asked to give a better view

Some organizations will only monitor numbers about 'delivery progress', risk or financials, ignoring the data that tells us whether all the work is contributing to better service performance (or not). You can use the ideas in this chapter to start conversations and to find others to work with to develop more productive and practical performance indicators.

Prototype a service dashboard
One tactic that's usefully provocative is to invent and prototype a 'service performance dashboard' that shows what leadership would ideally know and be looking at. You could do this for one important service or for a collection of them.

Populate it with real numbers, best guesses or fake examples, or leave it blank and ask others to guess. Casually show it to individuals. Take it to a board meeting. Add it to presentations and reporting slide decks. Leave a note with it on someone's desk and ask if they'd be interested in seeing the actual numbers. Point to it in meetings where delivery work is being discussed and ask what impact the work is likely to have on these critical indicators.

Summary

① Service performance is about how well it works for users, for operations and for the outcomes of the organization.

② Translate insight about users into performance indicators by flipping issues and 'anti-user needs' into what we'd see happen differently if it worked really well.

③ Measure and evaluate services by their effectiveness (purpose, user needs, outcomes) as well as their efficiency (time, cost, effort).

④ Identify ratios that represent what you should see increasing or decreasing as a service improves.

⑤ Not having an exact number is not the same as knowing nothing at all. You can often deduce or triangulate something from what you do have, even if that's an approximation or an educated guess.

⑥ Don't wait to be asked. Go ahead and show people what they should be looking at.

Proving the benefits of service transformation
A regulator's licencing service, UK

The £74 billion university research and biosciences industry in the UK relies on licences being granted effectively, so that establishments can carry out scientific research. There were problems with the regulator's legacy licencing service, including

- inefficient workflows, such as staff having to manually copy lengthy text into other formats to issue a licence;
- no single source of truth, which meant users could be looking at an outdated version of a licence;
- restrictions that prevented applications from being shared securely within the legacy system, increasing the risk of them being shared by other channels;
- constraints on account management – accounts were managed by a third-party supplier; and
- guidance that wasn't clear, so users didn't know what to include in licence applications, which increased the

number of revisions that had to be made, which was time consuming for everyone; and

- the legacy service didn't meet the UK government's service standard.[6]

A team was established to make the whole licencing service simpler, clearer and faster for users and establishments while increasing efficiency for the regulator.[7] This would include the parts that users see and interact with as well as the tools that staff used to process applications and issue licences.

To get this right, the team defined service performance measures, so that they and others would know to what extent they had achieved the desired outcomes for each step in the service. They worked closely with external users and operational staff, learning about the context, and testing different options, to develop a service that works for the many different research contexts.

The team engaged with 61% of the establishments involved in this form of research over three years. They built a service map showing how the service could work in future to help guide work along the right path. And senior leaders backed their evidence-based approach, which meant the team could focus on developing a service that worked well for all users, not just the more influential or vocal establishments.

The new service was established on time (meaning the legacy service did not need to be reprocured) and on budget, and it met the UK government's service standard. It continues to be developed and there are signs of success, including

- a 50% reduction in the number of iterations of draft project licence applications, reducing the burden on scientists assessing applications;
- a 50% reduction in the time taken to process a personal licence application, freeing up staff time for other work;

- a 30% decrease in the resources needed to answer parliamentary and freedom-of-information requests; and
- an increase in the percentage of users who are satisfied with the service, from 47% in 2018 to 78% in 2020, and a rise in people's confidence in the regulator's ability to provide an effective service.

From task measurement to whole-service performance KPIs
HM Passport Office, UK
HM Passport Office is the issuer of UK passports and is responsible for civil registration services in England & Wales through the General Register Office.

Colin Foley, the organization's head of business and service design, describes how service metrics were developed to guide decisions and the work of teams.[8]

Measuring the time taken for customers to receive a passport or a decision end to end is an important performance indicator that guides the work of many teams. Initially we needed to work from averages based on existing reports; it wasn't stored somewhere that we could work directly with. We needed data from people, from suppliers, and that was the challenge – we learned to put this in supplier contracts from the start.

Changing how we think about service measurement was part of a shift in mindset from individual functions doing individual tasks to us all being proactive about spotting and solving problems at every level. From 'I create this many items of work in a queue' to 'this customer has called 3 times so there's clearly a problem'. We all need that clarity and the data at a suitably granular level so that operational team leaders can think how best to coach staff, how to help people handle customer queries effectively or intervene with errors, and maintain and protect progress from end to end. It's very much a work in progress in terms of implementing these changes, but having clarity about service performance has set the vision for the step change we need from our business performance systems in future.

Counting the cost of service failure
Local government planning services

Charlie wanted to develop a loft extension to create a second bedroom in her apartment. She knew that home improvements don't need full planning permission. Other people have done similar conversions on her street so she hired an architect to draw up plans. The planning rules are complicated and the application process takes a long time. After waiting for months, Charlie is frustrated with the decision that the application is invalid. It has wasted time, money and effort for everyone: Charlie, her architect and the planning team.

As one director of planning explains: 'Around half of the planning applications we receive ... are found to be invalid – mostly because people have difficulty interpreting the complex planning requirements to make valid applications.'[9]

Estimating the cost, cumulative time and error rate of a service makes it clear what needs to be prioritized for improvement. In this case, it's the 'find out', 'choose' and 'apply' steps in the service, and the underlying guidance, rules and regulations.

Test and learn to improve steps in a service
Peek Vision

Peek Vision is a social enterprise that works with eye-health providers in low- and middle-income countries to optimize their services.[10]

A good eye-health service means that as many of a population as possible receive eye tests, and that those who need treatment are offered it – and receive it. This entails having enough people to conduct the tests, community leaders to encourage people to get tested, as well as communication and coordination to make sure people get to appointments for treatment.

Peek Vision provides the tools and processes that measure efficiency, effectiveness and equity across services. This helps eye-health providers to see where there is drop-out or problems with reach. They can then take specific action to improve the overall performance. Pilot studies using Peek Vision help potential funders and providers to model the likely impact of offering eye-health services in new regions.

The result is better vision and eye health for the millions of people worldwide who need it, and the evidence base that ensures the maximum value for the funding of such services.

Using service performance to challenge requests for new investment

Requests for team and project funding can be made by numerous people in large organizations. For budget holders and decision makers, it's not always easy to determine which are the right things to fund and support. Requests are submitted in varying styles, with different ways of describing benefits.

Decision makers will often agree to fund one team's request only to find out that another team is doing similar things in the same area, with a slightly different focus.

One leader began to challenge each team who asked for funding to first demonstrate they understood what good performance looked like across their four main services. At a weekly work review meeting, they would bring a printout of an example service performance dashboard and ask: 'Tell me how your idea is going to move the dial most on this and why you believe that. And then tell me what this number actually is, because I don't have it yet. And if you can't, go away and come back when you can.'

Chapter 4

Shape work and projects for success

Few people can predict which is the one legitimate option of all those available in a complex service environment.

Having established what good looks like, it's time to look at how to give new work and investment the direction or 'shape' to influence its success, so that it results in better-performing services.

Many organizations talk about the need for empowered teams, but this requires clarity of vision as well as other supportive conditions if teams are to have the best chance of delivering significant value. And that involves everyone being clear about the context, the problem to solve, the parameters or boundaries, the priorities and the realities of the organization and its users – which doesn't just happen by itself.

Getting involved in how new work starts is a lever for steering it towards better-performing services. In some organizations, a team will carry out an exploration (sometimes called 'discovery') to learn, and to generate, test or even invalidate ideas. Taking this approach can give good shape to work by default. But this typically only happens in some parts of the organization, and it requires experienced teams. The reality is that in a large organization, new work is started in many different ways, by different people.

When new investment is shaped in a way that dictates from the start what must be built or implemented, it can conceal what were other legitimate options and restrict what can be learned by 'doing'. This is especially true if this work is shaped or led by people who have not had recent operational experience, or experience of customers and users, or even of how modern delivery teams work.

Technology or design choices can be the easy part. Figuring out the rules, the ownership of data, the relationships or agreements necessary for organizations to share information or make systems work well together is often a real drawback. Teams might need to start collating data they don't normally need to collate. Entanglement of work in and between large organizations is the reality, which means projects can't always be neatly scoped up front. How we shape work and support teams to address these issues defines their success.

That said, organizations will always know some things up front. And there will always be important areas we won't know enough about. Organizational or political context also shapes the reality of what is possible, or prudent, at any given time. Developing the right 'story' about the work so that these elements can be woven together can be instrumental to its success.

This chapter will help you to set teams up with the best chance of doing something valuable, quickly.

Shape the problems to solve and the work to be done

There is a lot of good advice about how to frame work well.[1] The five points that follow are simple, but they can be used to plan quite complex changes, or to pragmatically explore new ideas.

1. Why do it?
2. Who is it for?

3. What does it mean for customers and users?
4. How will we know if it's worth it?
5. What are the potential problems?

1. Why do it?
The need to do something can be triggered by a significant opportunity or problem, a change in the market or in politics, or someone having a new idea. The first step is to understand the logic or rationale.

- What is this work about and what's the motivation? For example, is it a new legislative or regulatory change? An important contractual arrangement that's ending? An opportunity to make a better service?
- Why do this now? Why should this be a priority ahead of other opportunities? For example, perhaps we only have twelve months to bring a currently outsourced capability in-house; or maybe it's been prioritized because it's likely to have the single biggest impact on an important issue.
- Who wants this to happen? Whose problem is it? For example, it could be that of the senior accounting officer responsible for auditing payments; or of operations, who need better tools for decision making; or of a service team that wants to address significant inefficiency.
- What do we know? What are we assuming? What evidence is there that it is worth tackling this instead of something else? Assess the logic and rationale for it: 'We believe that doing x will result in y.'
- What problems will we solve and what opportunities are presented for the organization? For example:

  - making a service more efficient to operate;
  - developing a new capability that will improve or speed up the work of many teams;
  - better achieving policy outcomes by increasing uptake by customers and users;

- having greater transparency and control over finance and budgets;
- improving the accuracy of the data we base major decisions on; or
- reducing the time it takes to recover from critical and unplanned technology outages.

- What's our certainty level that we can – and should – do something impactful, and what evidence do we have? Have we prototyped and tested it with real users, or with operations, or with live data? Have we a plan for how to do so?

2. Who is it for?
This is about how the work is likely to help or benefit people or organizational goals, and who will be affected by it.

- Is this for external customers and users? Internal users? Individuals, groups, communities, businesses, the economy, the environment, climate or society? How many people are, or might be, involved?
- Who else is affected? For example, suppliers, third parties, staff behind the scenes or on the front line, managers of other functions, customer contact centres.
- What outcomes might others get? Being able to trust that the data they have about someone is accurate, say? Or being able to guide someone to the option that's best for them? Or being better able to answer the questions that people have?

3. What does it mean for customers and users?

- What does this mean for the people who will be impacted or for the people using the service? What is it that we present externally that people would have to understand or do, or that they might want to use or interact with?

- What problems or opportunities will we solve for customers and users? What will be better, or what will happen that didn't happen before?
- How does it relate to the main services the organization provides? Alternatively, how does it affect the individual stages within them? What are people doing, or trying to do, that this relates to? For example, it might be to do with renting a property, proving someone has had a vaccination, or buying a new home. Or perhaps it's to do with finding out what options are available, or the time spent waiting for a decision.

4. How will we know if it's worth it?

- What criteria would we use to evaluate it?
- What can we look at or measure to check we're on the right path?
- At what level do we care about value? Is this short term, medium term or longer term? Are we expecting a project-level or whole-service outcome? Or is it a capability that will increase the value of other teams or capabilities?

5. What are the potential problems?

- What are the potential problems with doing what we're doing? Do we understand any relevant ethical, inclusivity, privacy, security, inequity or sustainability issues?
- What's the potential impact if this turns out to be unsuccessful or wrong? Is it uncertain, huge and high profile? Or maybe it won't matter if it's wrong because the effect will be very small or because we'll learn what's more right?
- If we see it's not working, can we build in the ability to iterate or move away from it? How else do we mitigate the risk of being stuck with it, unable to make changes? Will we be able to make substantive improvements on a regular basis?

The five prompts above acknowledge that you know less at the beginning of a piece of work, but they allow teams to get started with good enough information anyway. They don't pretend or assume that everything is known. The answers to the questions above and the evidence gathered by simply making a start take the place of complicated specifications up front. The answers can help to create space to consider alternative approaches, for an uncertain project that's been timeboxed to deliver a fixed output.

You can get all the way through some project descriptions without them saying what the project is, who it's for or why it's happening. Write descriptions of work for the executive who only has a few minutes. Work on the answers as a whole team. Share the description with stakeholders and specialists to invite their input. In some cases you won't know the answers up front, and you won't be able to get full consensus. But you can still use the clarity these prompts provide as a tool for consent to get on with something.

Challenge the hidden assumptions that constrain the design

When developing or improving a service, there are always assumptions baked in about how it needs to operate – including assumptions that aren't well founded or that aren't true any more. These beliefs can end up dictating a method or shape to the work that results in inefficiencies or major problems. We don't want to miss or discard an opportunity to think in very different ways about what came before.

To reveal the opportunities to rethink from first principles, identify a few of the most significant assumptions together as a group – and then suggest how things could work entirely differently. Phillipa Elworthy (Department for Work & Pensions) suggests going first and being incredibly bold, to give others encouragement to do the same. Some examples include:

- rather than asking people to apply for something, give them the funding, access or permission automatically;
- rather than asking people to contact you to make an insurance claim, take action proactively whenever a triggering event occurs;
- rather than asking applicants to prove their identity and credit with documents and records that some won't have, authorize them automatically and put other controls in place to mitigate the risk.

Watch out that this doesn't just create an endless list of challenging ideas at different levels, which is easily done and is not helpful. Guide people towards identifying the options that are fundamental to a successful service, or the ones that are the root causes of major problems or costs.

Develop a consensus view about which of these options could have the most impact, and where the evidence we have about feasibility or viability doesn't rule it out (yet). These are the ripest for challenge.

The next step is to work through what the alternatives could be, and what would need to change for these to become reality. For example, we might need to let people 'soft check' their eligibility before applying, which would mean working with legal and compliance teams to change operating procedures. Or if we need to accept the risk of not authenticating people, we would have to think creatively about how to work with local communities to validate a claim instead. This might mean working with risk teams, the board and the regulators to change the rules.

Some teams organize assumptions and alternatives into themes and then vote on the strongest ideas, or compare the impact and certainty of each. What results from this process are options that can be worked up as an immediate set of priorities for a new team to investigate. At the very least it helps to test out parameters and to assess where a team can and cannot challenge the thinking with leadership and other stakeholders.

How to protect what matters

Some things are immovable, whatever the priorities are. These are what *must* be true or *must not* happen. Without having these in place, people can feel uncomfortable that something important could be missed in the drive towards the boldest possible vision of the service.

In some situations we need to stand up a service as quickly as possible, with the absolute minimum needed to operate. This could be due to urgency – something we all experienced during the pandemic – or because it can be a good way to derisk major new service development: that is, to learn by operating a very simple version of a service with very small numbers of users to start with, and not lumbering it from the start with complicated rules, features or technology that might not be necessary.

But if iterative ways of working aren't built in from the start, important things can be left undone or can be done badly, and then never prioritized or resolved. Some examples:

- A simple version of a service is created initially to only work online, but that results in excluding some of the people who need to use it.
- An online application form and process are designed to be clearer, simpler and faster, but they don't meet the current finance and accounting rules and checking compliance is time consuming.
- A capability is delivered 'on time and on budget' but it doesn't meet important standards set by the organization, by the government or by regulators, stakeholders or ethics boards.

Committing to a plan that protects the time and space to continue to develop and iterate means that a team can revisit choices like these, whether they were a quick (bad) starting point to learn from or arose from an unforeseen situation. But the risk is that the work needed is never (re)prioritized. So stating 'truths' that must or must not happen can provide anchors for teams, and help to reassure leadership. It protects what is out of bounds or must be done, while leaving everything else up for grabs.

Reality requires compromise

There are times when we all have to compromise and make (or forgive) difficult decisions and tradeoffs that we all know will affect how well a service works. It's an uncomfortable but unavoidable part of putting to work our experience and skills to make something valuable in a real-life context. Few of us are here to deliver some abstract ideal in a vacuum, so it's just as important to understand and allow for the times when compromise is necessary. That said, it's hard to know when to stand your ground and when to lend support for (or at least go along with) options that are not ideal but that are potentially unavoidable. What's important is to do as much as possible to

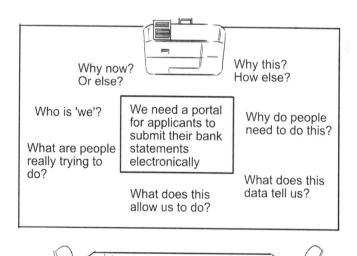

Figure 7. Unpack the beliefs and rationale behind 'the solution'. (Shared with permission from Ayesha Moarif.)

understand and communicate the implications; to collectively decide the 'red lines' for yourself, the service or the organization; to protect the ability to evolve from this situation in future; and to then forgive yourself and any others who turn up to make the tough calls.

Bringing constructive challenge to a predetermined project
If a specific option is predetermined in a way that seems risky or doesn't appear to address any known problems, ask questions to uncover the logic and rationale behind it. Find out which alternative options that seem legitimate have been considered and assess what's missing. This activity will either strengthen the rationale for the current approach (and you can often then help teams communicate this more clearly) or it can expose other ways to deliver better value for money.

Position the work to improve services

Disjointed pieces of delivery are one reason why whole services don't perform as well as they should. When there are dozens or even hundreds of teams, an important and valuable skill is to be able to take individual requests for change and figure out how to test or deliver them, given the complexity and all the other work in play – whether that's to merge the work, to wait, to say no, or to change scope. Large organizations need people who are able to do this and who have experience of users, operations and modern ways of working. We need ways to see the big picture while working at a detailed enough level to be able to understand the work in progress, to see how to reduce fragmentation and to help teams figure out sensible ways to deliver changes across complicated portfolios.

Chapter 2 included ways to map work in progress across stages in services, and chapter 3 looked at how to measure performance. Together, these things provide a framework for shaping work to result in better end-to-end services.

From replacing IT to making whole services perform better
Work is often underway to replace or 'refresh' older IT systems, and to fix problems with how data is structured or stored and with how systems 'talk' to each other. This is legitimate and important work that can hugely improve services under certain conditions: when it follows good practice for modern technology, when it isn't done in isolation away from the reality of use, and when it improves the ability and speed of being able to make changes.

The focus on replacing IT is riskier when the teams involved can't say what a good outcome looks like for the part of services that technology supports. Particularly if, at the same time, someone is pushing for creating or buying in monolithic chunks of technology. If there's just a list of features or requirements in abstract – rather than the reality of what's important to users, what good outcomes look like, and a way to test and learn what will work best – it's easier to assume that any procured off-the-shelf solution will do the job. But genuine IT modernization is not about adding or replacing bits of technology, it is about increasing the value that technology and capability bring. This book should help you clarify what that value is, in practical terms.

The service list, service framework and performance indicators covered in chapters 1–3 will give valuable context to many pieces of work. They also give the basis of stronger success criteria.

Assess all the legitimate options
It's easy to assume that technology is the answer, even though it is often policy or procedural complexity or data ownership issues that make a service hard to operate or to use.

To redesign how we process applications for financial support, for example, we could assume that we need to replace the underlying case management system. But we could also

- remove complexity from the policy;
- simplify the criteria and standards for evidence;

- find a clearer, simpler way for people to know how to prove their entitlement;
- clean up historical data to make the process less error prone;
- develop a tool that includes a checklist for internal users on how to verify entitlement; or
- automate checks of basic data so that verification happens before an application is submitted.

Teams and individuals should be able to say why they're adopting one approach over another. It should be easy to relate this rationale back to how the problem and opportunity are described; if it's not, then either it's the wrong problem, we've learned something important, or it's the wrong solution.

Supporting capabilities, not commodities

All that said, creating entirely bespoke ways of designing and supporting services can be inefficient if a commodity solution could be used to do it well enough. Or if, because of what it does or how it's being used, it just doesn't matter that much.

But what a commodity is rather depends on the purpose and value of services. For service organizations in many countries, electricity from a national grid would be a commodity no one would consider recreating. How to better support access to it for electric vehicles in different countries and contexts requires testing, learning and iterating. And in lower-income countries, services for very rural populations may require their own electricity generation.

So although there *are* some similarities in what's needed – between people, as well as services – we often don't know enough *up front* about what that means for the context, or about what the impact of choosing or constraining the options will be.

To create or choose genuinely supporting capabilities you need to know

- what's needed and what good looks like in terms of outcomes and performance, not just requirements, features or abstract processes;
- how to make capabilities that are usable, findable, inclusive and responsive to changing needs, as well as how they contribute to or affect overall service performance (bearing in mind that some supporting capabilities are based on technology that people use to do tasks while others handle tasks on behalf of people); and
- how to set them up to iterate towards what good looks like wherever appropriate, i.e. how to make capabilities that do a better job of supporting services, or that are more trustworthy, transparent, secure or reliable.

There are many examples of technology, products, designs and capabilities that are good at doing what's needed for a given service stage and are iterated according to collective priorities. 'Software as a service' is an entire sector. 'Government as a platform' is a move to create modern foundations to underpin many public services: GOV.UK's 'Notify' and 'Pay' are two widely used examples.[2] The authors of Team Topologies, Matthew Skelton and Manuel Païs, invented 'independent service heuristics', which are rules of thumb to help identify candidates for these 'stand alone' capabilities.[3]

But in some organizations, the decisions to centralize technology choices are made entirely outside services, away from service teams, and at a distance from those who feel the impact of any poor choices. Separate technology or procurement workstreams can be incredibly risky for this reason.

Avoid constraining what you need to learn
Modern technology approaches mean arranging to be able to learn and improve as you go. There are good examples of organizations taking a more nuanced approach to choosing when and

how to use technologies across the organization, including how well it serves what customers and users ultimately try, want or need to do, and how well it can adapt to what we learn when it doesn't work well. Hackney Council's IT 'tech radar',[4] for example, allows it to test and introduce new technology in a way that allows teams to explore what's best for the context, while still monitoring, maturing and standardizing architecture and technology choices.

There are huge benefits in being able to quickly buy in standard capabilities to spin up or test something – if you can avoid the potential pitfalls. But the minute you're constrained by the choices made, whether that's by reusing legacy technology or by the decision to procure software, you're not learning what's needed about the problems to solve and the biggest risks; you're learning about technology instead.

Handling challenge

It won't be obvious to everyone why it's useful to unpack and describe work in the way that this chapter describes. People can be accustomed to deciding what's needed up front and telling a team what the scope is. For them, the activities described here might seem like a waste of time. They might worry about the 'effect' on delivery plans or projections, without realizing that those delivery plans were on shaky ground to begin with if they haven't given due consideration to the legitimate options.

It's safest to start by asking what consideration has been given to other options or other ways to scope the work for success. There might be good answers. By framing the problem well, you're not putting anything at risk: you are bringing it one step closer to reality, which will hit at some point anyway and it's better to deal with it sooner rather than later. At the very least, a clear description means that more people will understand what's intended.

Summary

① Shape work by setting out what we already know, while creating the mandate to learn about what we don't. Why do it? Who is it for? What does it means for users? How will we know it's worth it? What are the potential problems?

② Reduce the risk by identifying the biggest assumptions influencing the service for which there's not good evidence. Set out what needs to change to be able to handle these differently.

③ Steer changes to technology away from meeting abstract requirements and towards what will give value in terms of service performance and outcomes, with the ability to iterate over time.

Changing policy to remove barriers to service delivery

The Department for Environment, Food & Rural Affairs, UK: services for farmers and landowners

The Department for Environment, Food & Rural Affairs (DEFRA) is responsible for improving and protecting the environment, growing a green economy, and supporting the food production, farming and fishing industries in the UK.

The Future Farming programme is providing regular income for farmers to improve the environment and food production as part of their farm business, as well as funding for farmers to invest in technology, equipment and innovation.

Rohan Gye is deputy director and service owner. Below he talks about how sometimes you can't design a service that works well unless you change the policy.[5]

> We are often asked whether for us as a programme it is all about designing for user needs. But it isn't; at least not directly.

Sometimes you need to fix the policy to be able to open up the opportunities to deliver a service well. Which isn't answering a user's needs exactly, but it's removing the barriers to a better service for everyone involved.

For example, traditional schemes had been open for a 12-week window in the annual farming cycle during which farmers could make applications for funding to deliver environmental outcomes. But farmers are busy. And at different times of the year. So inevitably we would receive the bulk of applications in the final week, causing a bottleneck. Not just in processing the applications, but also in handling all the questions and anxiety around whether this situation met those criteria and so on. It put huge pressure on operations; it caused stress and anxiety for farmers. There's no 'service design' that can help with that, except to remove the 12-week window and be able to accept applications throughout the year – which required a change in policy.

It took a lot of effort and influence to change, but we did it. Farmers and landowners can now apply at any time. There was a huge sigh of relief because the first new funding options were made available to farmers at harvest time – we had an unexpected early harvest this year. So for everyone to apply within that 12-week window would have been difficult.

The fact that people can apply at any time now means that we can learn, iterate and then roll options out more widely as we go. We don't have to make things available to everyone from day one in a 'big bang' way. We can test with a small number of people. Then expand to a wider cohort. And then only grow from there when we're fully satisfied that it works – for our external users, and critically our operational users too. And that builds in safety and reassurance for everyone.

We no longer have to roll out multiple entirely new standards that everyone also needs to learn all at once, just to coincide with application windows. We can introduce new options as and when they're ready, test them before we expand, and do it at a time that makes sense, avoiding the busiest farming months.

Challenging assumptions that dictate a delivery approach

Millions of people worldwide have to recertify that they're still eligible for benefits once they're receiving them. It's a common assumption that this is the only legitimate way to operate these kinds of services. The impact of this choice, or whether this is the only option, often isn't explored. Instead of helping people to get or keep the money or support they're entitled to, it's assumed that everyone will continue to claim what they aren't entitled to. But this approach doesn't just affect the people that need support and the time and effort it takes them to recertify each time (and those that don't get what they need as a result). It also has a huge impact on the decision-making process, the operations, the people who work on cases, and the cost and avoidable demand of operating this way.

One US state was working on changes to family and medical leave during the pandemic. It was initially assumed that people would have to recertify weekly that they still needed benefits. The teams working with legislators had to help everyone understand the cost in terms of the caseworking teams' time of taking this approach, and also make it clear that it meant that families with infants would have to prove every week that they still have a newborn baby: 'We asked them what, specifically, they were trying to prevent?'[6]

Rethinking 'creditworthiness' to offer services to more people
Mahindra Finance

When Mahindra Finance[7] expanded their vehicle financing service to people in rural areas of India, it meant challenging assumptions about creditworthiness. These new customers would be unbanked, with no identity documents. Their cashflow might be unpredictable. Lending money to these people would be unthinkable to many finance companies operating in other countries. Mahindra Finance had to develop radically different ways to handle the design of loans, approval, repayment terms and branch locations, as well as needing to support collection in cash.[8] It needed to recruit workers that could speak local dialects, who would be in the right position to assess local situations. This meant changing the way decisions were made to support decentralized approvals. Their focus on helping rural citizens improve their lives kept them on path. Mahindra Finance today serves 50% of villages in India and has 6 million customers.

Failing to see the impact of internal change on service performance
Family workers in local government
When the work to change an internal system is shaped without regard for improving the services it supports, it can fail in significant ways. Jane works with families in local government. She was hired for six months to progress a large backlog of cases: real families who were struggling. The family rooms are downstairs and the computers are upstairs. Jane has to log on and use three different IT systems to record details and update records. This takes around 20 minutes for every client and it has to be done after each session, vastly reducing the time available and restricting the number of clients Jane can see 'even if I run up and down the stairs'. At an 'IT refresh' meeting it was announced they were moving to a new 'one stop shop'. Jane asked if it's called that because it will just be one system to log onto now – 'The man just laughed at me'. Whatever the goal of this 'refresh' was, it didn't appear to get families the help they needed any faster, and it didn't save time or cost for council staff who worked with them– despite the imperative to reduce the backlog.

Chapter 5

Make policy that delivers better service outcomes

Helping policymakers, technologists, operational staff and designers to work together effectively is one obvious step, but it's not simply about including more people – the entire approach is evolving.

This chapter looks briefly at what the public sector organizations that are taking a modern approach to policymaking are doing, and who is involved. Modern policymaking processes help to 'frontload' the risk of doing or building the wrong thing, by organizing to learn about and continue to adapt to real-life context, behaviour and outcomes. This means that teams only take forward the ideas and options that carry the most legitimacy, and they organize themselves to continue to develop and evolve policy to improve outcomes, where it's worth doing so.

A huge amount of public policy relates to services. Yet service delivery and operations are treated separately to many policymaking processes, increasing the risk that policies don't work, don't work well, have a negative impact, or miss opportunities. Our goal is to close the gap to more quickly and safely learn what we need to know about reality before significant commitments are made and options are locked down.[1] Use the guide in chapter 3 to define policy intent and measurable service outcomes to establish what a service ideally does. It's the start of a conversation about evaluating and improving policy through services.

This isn't a new idea, but it's also still early days as policymaking evolves for the digital era. Practical ideas and examples are being shared by the UK public policy design community (currently sponsored by the UK government's policy profession[2]) and can be found in the work of James Plunkett (a digital, data and technology leader and the author of *End State*[3]) and Cat Drew (the Design Council's chief of design and co-founder of the UK government's Policy Lab[4]) among others. Denmark's Agency for Digital Government has published guidance for how to make what it calls 'digital-ready legislation'.[5] This includes simpler and unambiguous rules that can be more easily implemented into services and potentially automated where that's appropriate.

'Frontload' the risk of new or changing policy

Research shows that there are three aspects to policymaking that help to increase confidence and reduce risk and to set up organizations for better-performing services with improved outcomes.

1. Set the intent

This part involves setting out what we believe about what we're trying to achieve. An initial decision to do or change something (or a political manifesto) means that policy people need to fully understand the underlying intent and the potential implications, engaging with stakeholders to begin to test the validity of a policy, the reaction to it, the potential support for it, the issues surrounding it or the impact of it. This means creating the relevant arguments and logic, and testing and iterating them, while analysing the existing evidence base.

There's not so much that's different about how this part works in modern policymaking, except perhaps for what it doesn't do. It doesn't – or shouldn't promise to – do anything if the evidence base just isn't there or if there are other priorities. And it should avoid at all costs promising to deliver something very specific from the outset – such as an app, a portal or a database – as the only legitimate 'solution'.

2. Iterate policy by learning about the reality

This activity explores and refines some of the options and parameters that are more likely to result in the desired outcome. It sets out to learn what's useful to know now or to know quickly, that won't unhelpfully constrain all the legitimate delivery options later.

At this point, organizations working to improve their policy outcomes are generally doing the following.

- They tend to be working closely with the people affected by the policy. This includes everything from ensuring the team itself is made up of people the policy affects, to wider engagement with more of the people affected, to involving users and communities directly in decisions and making the hard trade-offs together (sometimes called 'co-design'). At the very least, they will be testing and iterating ideas with people early on.
- They should be including those with recent experience of the reality of operations, of users, of technology and of modern delivery practices. The creation of modern 'policy design' teams typically includes a wider set of disciplines than the traditional economists, scientists and lawyers, including professions such as service designers, technologists, security experts and user researchers.
- They are usually working in the open, so that others know what's happening and why, and have the chance to provide

constructive challenge. They should be timeboxing efforts to focus on priorities, such as establishing a fortnightly rhythm of learning, testing and iterating, and they are likely to be using social media, writing blog posts and sharing progress publicly.

- They tend to be 'prototyping' and communicating ideas to test with users in different contexts, developing or modelling example scenarios, and exploring which factors influence how the policy might work.

At this point, it's about establishing the facts that set the parameters, and not about dictating how something is done or making overly optimistic assumptions about how people will behave.

So it might be safe to explore some 'objective'(ish) aspects up front – such as modelling pricing, incentives or changes to taxation; the scientific basis of options; researching what would make a proposition attractive enough to achieve take-up goals; or analysing the size of the opportunity. And in doing this, you'll likely receive input and feedback from a wider range of interested parties, lobbyists and stakeholders that could be more subjective, but also potentially influential. But it still isn't realistic or safe to assume that a solution – say, a mobile app – will be used by everyone successfully, or that a simple decision tree can be created and used to determine everyone's business circumstances in such a way that they are able to self-serve digitally.

Importantly, this phase could still conclude that a policy isn't workable, isn't worthwhile, has a negative impact, or isn't worth doing yet – and this is what makes it valuable to investigate up front and not when it's too late. There are plenty of examples where disaster and embarrassment have been avoided by changing course, particularly where technology, security, data and design awareness is less accessible to those driving policy ideas.

3. Develop and evolve policy by operating in reality

There's only so much that can be learned up front without trying it in practice. But the handoffs in traditional policymaking separate the people who are 'thinking and deciding' from those who are 'doing and delivering'. When it's important to get it right, organizations need the people who have experience of complex service environments and of users and the people with experience of policymaking to be learning and evolving things together.

That said, when legislation changes, some services will simply need to adjust to incorporate or reflect new laws and procedures, e.g. changes to payment or taxation levels or frequency, or to offer greater protection of privacy. There are many 'good practice' principles to consider in the digital era that don't always need to be learned about from scratch, they just need to be applied. Denmark's Agency for Digital Government has guidance for changing legislation, given that many services will be digitally enabled. It includes the requirements to make the rules as simple as possible, to follow good practice standards, and to focus on how feasible policy is to implement (including the potential for automating aspects of case processing) and on how it will be administered on an ongoing basis:

> It … requires the civil service to draw the attention of politicians to the fact that exceptions and ambiguities may be politically desirable now, but may constitute an obstacle to the operation of the law as intended later, for example, because of a more expensive and more risky implementation.[6]

In other cases, policy development and iteration (or 'operationalization') need to be integral parts of delivery, because this is where ideas meet reality: creating or significantly evolving a service, changing the criteria or standards of evidence, adjusting how individual parts of an existing service work.

Developing policy for new services

Rather than having all the answers, complexity and edge cases (that are potentially wrong) built in from the start, the less risky approach can be to find answers to policy questions that are 'good enough' for now, to then refine them and build in ways to scale or change them if needed, as you go.

Some services that started out very small, with controlled numbers of users to learn what works best, were able to do this by having a policymaker on hand. They could then make the ultimate decision about situations that hadn't yet been covered when they arose. This meant that teams could rapidly learn about all the other aspects of operating, starting with the simplest possible version of the policy, and they could more safely develop the rules and guidance once they'd learned more about everything else.

Evolving or changing policy for existing services

Map out what's already there in terms of services and then help others understand how effective each part is. Chapters 2 and 3 showed how to do this from the outside in. This is powerful for leaders, politicians and policymakers, as it reveals where in the system they can make incisive investments and evaluate returned value.

Some organizations develop a viewpoint of the whole service that gives policymakers a framework for seeing and understanding where and how policy affects how well a service works, the basis of the decisions being made, and what to bear in mind when considering changes.

It can be difficult to find the right people to care about the ongoing performance of policy. The emphasis is often more on developing new ideas or making changes than it is on improving what's already there. For large services you can play a valuable role in translating the changes organizations are often making (to policy, as well as to technology or operating procedure) into how these could improve overall service performance – or at least have a neutral effect rather than a negative one. For smaller services that aren't as high profile, or where there's no one who is obviously invested in it, you could seek performance data and assess the size of the opportunity and whether there is a compelling case to invest in it.

Improving services without needing to change the policy
There's often much that can be improved about a service without requiring any – or any significant – policy change at all. Despite the stories you might hear, how a policy works today isn't necessarily dictated by how that policy was written. Read the words of the policy. Ask the policymaker to run you through it. How a service works could be the result of historic context or working practice that people have interpreted as 'that's what the policy is', making it ripe for challenge. I've worked on many initiatives to operationally improve a service that were entirely within the remit of the existing policy.

Navigate shifts in decision-making power

This isn't a one-way street. By looking at service outcomes across the whole, idea generation should work both ways. Service teams and leaders are well positioned to propose ideas back to policymakers, politicians or executives based on the evidence the service provides. There are many compelling stories to tell about taking action to solve important problems and create opportunities for people, communities, constituents and taxpayers.

The more that influence and power is shared between people, users, groups and communities, the harder it is to balance trade-offs and make hard decisions for which there will never be consensus. But there are always useful questions to ask. What do we need to learn and get evidence about that would help steer us one way or another? Does a course of action go against important principles, morals, ethics or standards? How flexible and reversible is the commitment or course of action if we're wrong? What are the true constraints on what is possible in this situation? How can we undertake testing – in reality, with very small numbers – to learn what it takes to reduce risks?

Kiran Dhillon (an experienced design practitioner) emphasizes the relationship of politics to policy and told me:

> In reality, politics will influence policy making to varying degrees, sometimes requiring mediation between political choices and evidence. Ministers and political parties might be very prescriptive (and sometimes dogmatic) about the detailed design and implementation of a policy. In some cases, this is because they need to balance wider and possibly competing interests and priorities. In other cases, it might be because of political expediency or ideology. Ideally, we're still able to bring our experience and expertise to bear to help steer away from a course of action that won't have the intended outcomes nor represent value for money – and that could be very difficult to implement – and towards other options that are more likely to achieve the intention. However, the political environment might not always make this possible. Go easy on yourself and others in these situations.

What helps move everyone forward together is real skill and clarity in communication and translation of complex issues so that everyone can properly understand the constraints, the reality of any trade-offs, and the implications. This entails a culture that respects different perspectives and nuance – with enough support from the top for a faster 'good enough' decision to be taken, protecting the time and space to take action if that decision proves to be wrong.

Summary

① Organizations are changing the traditional policymaking process to be better positioned to learn, test and iterate to achieve the intent when the policy meets the reality.

② There are three parts to modern policymaking:

- setting intent,
- iterating policy by learning about reality and testing options, and
- developing and evolving policy by operating in the real world.

③ A wider set of disciplines are becoming involved in making good policy, particularly those experienced in service delivery, technology, security, product, user-centred design and operations.

④ Don't try to answer all the questions up front. Build in safe ways of continuing to develop policy as part of delivering a new service or changing an existing one.

⑤ Safer to explore up front are the facts and the parameters. This could include modelling aspects, such as the characteristics of a population, pricing, incentive levels or taxation amounts. Although behavioural aspects are better explored with service delivery teams, who have practical skills to help test and learn about the reality and nuance of the individual users and people affected.

⑥ Many existing operational services can be radically improved without the need to change policy.

Developing and improving policy and services together

The Department for Education, England: Teacher Services

The Department for Education (DfE) is responsible for children's services and education, including early years provision, schools, higher and further education policy, apprenticeships and wider skills in England.

This includes responsibility for teaching: who teaches, what gets taught, to whom and how. An important part of this is providing services to people who teach and to people who could become teachers.

Rachel Hope is the former service owner for Teacher Services and Pete Ward is the current deputy director. Below they describe how they organized policy design and service delivery to orient teams around mutual learning and iteration.[7]

This approach has reduced the internal friction where one team 'owns' the technology and data, another 'owns' the analysis, and another is accountable for outcomes, which so often leads to disjointed services and internal tensions. At DfE it has led to services that improve the experiences for users, increase the recruitment and retention of teachers, and reduce costs for schools as well as DfE.

When we started, there was a handoff between policy formation and service delivery. This meant you had 'lock in', where the learning stops, an idea becomes fixed, and you're no longer in a position to grow or iterate. There were different understandings of success, and pressures coming from different places.

This began to change when DfE established a single service owner role with responsibility for policy as well as service delivery. This meant a service owner was responsible for the outcomes being achieved, regardless of the function – policy, delivery or operations.

As an end-to-end service owner, you hear and understand the pressures faced by different teams and individuals. Policy designers had pressure from stakeholders and ministers. Delivery and frontline teams had pressure from users, as well as needing to understand the delivery infrastructure, and about what was possible or safe to do. When these pressures are in conflict, it's incredibly hard for anyone to prioritize overall. Your job is to make sure that you're all working on the right problems, that you're able to deliver at pace, and that teams can iterate what they do as learning grows. We did three things to address this.

Firstly, we established a single vision of teaching services, based on a map of all of the 'service lines' [collections of related services]. Each service line had clear outcomes and measurable goals. For example, for the 'become a teacher' service, it was about growth in numbers of people teaching. This clarity helped provide focus and cut through some of the opinion, in favour of evidence guided by learning, action and experimentation.

Secondly, we set up teams to be able to make changes to services quickly. We no longer have policy teams that are entirely separate to digital delivery teams, with handoffs between the two. Policy people are included in teams that deliver services. User-centred design and technology people are included in teams that create and iterate earlier stage policy. The policy people in digital teams are at daily standups and learning about digital ways of working. Product managers are wondering where does 'product' begin and end, realizing that perhaps they work in policy after all.

Parts of our services – or the reality that users experience – are split across how our organization is structured. Many of the teams involved will have their own different working practices. Rather than decide which 'way' or 'culture' is right or wrong, there has to be a new, collaboratively forged culture for people to work together across services.

So thirdly, we intentionally swap people around so they can better understand the perspectives of their colleagues. A member of the team may spend a year working on a service that is all about increasing the number of people applying for teacher training, and so advocating for teacher training candidates, before moving onto a service helping provide teachers with professional development. This diversity of experience is important to have a holistic and balanced view of our users. This doesn't just apply to services, but also roles. For example, a policy person might lead the prioritization of a service line backlog. Equally, a product person might talk with the minister about trade-offs. Very quickly, viewpoints shift, and everyone begins to see and to care about the success of the whole.

Early on, we found that language often got in the way of progress. Roadmaps could be interpreted as Gantt charts, or a simple 'now, next, later'. Some people felt uncomfortable with some agile or digital ways of working, such as using an ideas board. So we collectively decided to create our own language. For example, now we talk about 'bids' as the ideas for what we could do to gain more teachers, improve teaching or better support people to become great teachers. Bids involve ideas about policy, technology, data, user-facing design, analytics, how we structure teams or any other organizational capability. Bids can come from anyone in any team. Once they're collected, we do some analysis, and gather extra data and evidence where necessary to help us to collectively vote on these bids. We do this together, in the open, taking into account other priorities, which means everyone hears the rationale for why we might or might not take a bid forward. We initially had some feedback that this felt too top-down, so we iterated and improved on it. As with everything, the process needs to constantly improve.

Having the single view of policy and digital enables us to make small policy changes all the time to improve the service and the outcomes we're getting. For example, how many times can one applicant apply to be a teacher, having been rejected before? We can update the rules in the service to find out what works best. In this case, analysis in the initial four months after changing this rule shows that the offer rate where providers made a decision had improved by nine percentage points.

Integrating policy formulation and service delivery has been a journey over the last four years. We started in 2018. At the beginning, people did not understand each other's roles or did not appreciate who does what. For example, the difference between 'policy analysis' and 'business analysis'. But in 2022 we're now at a stage where there are business analysts and user researchers fully embedded in teams working on policy wherever it makes sense to.

We've been able to do this successfully because we started small. We didn't try to do or change everything all at once.

Originally we had just one team with a few policy and digital delivery people. We grew slowly, adding one more team. Then we used these two teams to seed people to grow other teams. We had senior-level support and advocacy from people at different levels throughout the organization and we couldn't have achieved what we have without that. We're now scaling much of this way of working to many other areas. It has become a model to follow and learn from, across the entire department.

Learning from reality results in more constructive conversations

The Department for Environment, Food & Rural Affairs, UK: services for farmers and landowners
Rohan Gye is deputy director and service owner of DEFRA's Future Farming programme. Below he talks about the programme's approach to policy development, which involves users, alongside assessments of feasibility, viability and desirability.[8]

As a programme we constantly talk to farmers, we work in the open, we share what we're doing and we learn and iterate before we scale anything. And we work hand in hand with digital, operational, policy and compliance specialists.

This way of working assures us that we can't go too far down the wrong path.

For example, a standard was being developed for farmers that sets out how to work towards improved soil quality. The feedback from co-design partners on this particular standard had been that it was great. So ordinarily, it would have passed through into delivery.

Because of how we work now, farmers were able to see what was being proposed at an early stage. They asked the people behind the standard: 'How will you actually be able to check whether we've improved organic matter in soil? You'd either have to ask us to prove it ourselves or you'd have to check the soil yourselves first, which is incredibly time consuming. So you're asking us to prove a result, without benchmarking it. So what's the actual value in what you're asking?'

For every single option or standard we try to introduce we have to ask: What are we asking users to do? Will we add or remove effort? Is it achievable? Is it measurable? If not, then it's all very well having 'recommendations', but for the people that have to check compliance or audit spend it's not particularly practical. And for farmers it's ambiguous. And when it's neither practical nor clear, it's not efficient.

This kind of analysis provides the basis for a more valuable and constructive conversation to have with everyone who is interested in, auditing, enabling or delivering changes to services, so that we can all move forwards together.

Chapter 6

Set service strategy to drive work

Some organizations won't realize the impact of a given approach on the success of a project, portfolio or programme. They run on a kind of default setting, which hinders learning.

I magine a friend who wants to make an app. Instead of coming up with an idea, a target audience and a tangible prototype to test, they just hire people who build 'an app'. Eventually they show it to a few people they think will like it only to have it pointed out that they have no idea how it would help them with anything. Strategy in larger, older organizations can sometimes feel like this.

For strategy to be effective, it needs clarity of vision that's ambitious enough to set future direction but practical enough to guide what teams actually do.

Strategy is useful when it has an opinion.[1] Rather than, say, talking about 'transformation' in general terms, a strategy should set out what an organization is transforming from and what it's working towards. If it's not clear what you get by changing, people will find it mysterious. A narrative that provides context and rationale makes it relatable. And telling a relatable story will make more sense to more people across the organization.

Strategy that includes parameters helps people and teams determine for themselves what's most important to learn and do while retaining some overarching control.

Without something or someone guiding the work, it can be chaotic, which then takes more time and effort to rescue.

This chapter gives you structure and examples for setting a clear strategy in four parts:

- stating the 'job' of a service;
- setting driving principles;
- choosing an approach that makes success more likely; and
- creating a clear narrative that tells the story.

Good service strategy

A good first step is to help everyone to know what the job of a service is, and use this to set the direction of travel.

The job of a service
The clearer it is what a service is there to do, the easier it is to know if it's doing it – or to anticipate what's needed to better achieve it. Chapter 3 provides a format to define the job of a service and its ideal outcomes as the basis for assessing its performance. This alone can be enough to prompt a change in strategy or approach, if a service isn't delivering the intent of the policy or if the rate of achieving desirable outcomes is low.

By defining the job of each of the main services, the big-picture prize becomes clearer for an entire organization, and this can give the underlying context to all the other work taking place, whether or not it is service related. What an organization achieves is a sum of all its parts. Examples are

- a social security system that works more successfully, with the right people managing to get support, or that helps more people into work more often, and sustainably, without difficulty; or
- a tax system that helps and encourages the right people to pay the right tax, while avoiding friction, pain, noncompliance and related problems.

Strong teams need direction
Adding a direction of travel over the top of what a service is there to do can help teams focus. Below I set out two examples.

We're creating the foundations to provide support for the next decade. We're not developing a one-off service for the current policy. We're creating the foundations for financial support far into the future. We're doing this by establishing the teams, the technology and the processes to make different kinds of payment, set up to be able to iterate and rapidly respond to new priorities.

This puts the focus on developing and maintaining enduring capabilities and teams that successive leadership teams would draw on (even if the intention changes), making the whole endeavour more future-proof – not because it somehow predicts the future, but because it is set up to handle change more easily.

Reduce our climate impact. Our services will be carbon neutral by 2030. This includes what our customers need to do to use those services, how our suppliers operate, and how we run and approach the constituent parts of our services.

This strategy provides a theme across many services. It gives a focus that individual teams can use to guide decision making and planning, prompting very different thinking from the current set up and ways of working.

Establish driving principles

There are often very different intentions and goals between people, professions and functions. Ideally, teams involved in services can judge for themselves the right actions to take, but this relies on people also knowing what's most important or valuable given the current bigger picture. It's hard to choose between options or make decisions to move on when there are mixed or conflicting messages from leadership.

A good way to achieve this is to agree driving principles for the services you work with – the kind that enable teams to make their own decisions, and ones that are also likely to meet overall priorities.

Let's look at four different kinds.

1. A single imperative
Lara Sampson (a partner at Public Digital[2]) introduced me to the idea of a single imperative, used as a forcing function when there's too much going on or where there is an overriding priority. It's a statement that is clear enough to drive the focus for the next phase (a time period of your choosing), beyond which it can change or expand. Examples:

- Pay people now, so they stay home during a pandemic.[3]
- Get as many people vaccinated as possible before winter, while prioritizing those who are vulnerable.

Even when there's a single imperative, it's not easy to hold the line. It needs to be constantly repeated and consistently adhered to, with all work and every decision compared against it on a daily basis. Doing this prevents it becoming a forced issue later on. Even if an organization can do it all, it's still healthy to have the absolute priority in mind.

2. One ambitious goal

Set a single, measurable, ambitious goal for the future.[4] One that's bold enough to be almost implausible. Then bring different people and specialisms together to figure out how to work towards it over time. Examples:

- Reduce the time it takes to issue a work permit from three weeks to twenty-four hours within the next five years.
- Reduce the cost to serve to ten cents for every dollar in the overall budget over the next twenty-four months.

This works best for mature services, where the emphasis can more safely shift to improving efficiency.

BBVA Compass made a long-term commitment to improve end-to-end banking experiences for customers,[5] including setting an ambitious goal for same-day decision making for offering a loan.[6] It took people and teams working together across the entire organization to bring this about.

This kind of strategy can serve everyone. It makes sense for the person who needs a loan – who can quickly find out if they're eligible and potentially receive money the same day – and it makes sense for the organization, who can start to earn interest on the loan sooner. It also sets the ambition to radically improve the operational tools and procedures that underpin a service.

3. Timeboxed focus

There could be a critical issue or a risk that is serious enough to override every other priority for a fixed period of time – recovering from a major cyber attack, for example. These events can radically change priorities overnight. Examples:

- For the next two years we're rebuilding our technology and data from the ground up and top down to make it simpler, safer, more reliable and more secure. We'll organize ourselves to be able to adapt and iterate our capabilities and processes, to deliver better services for our residents, businesses and users, sustainably.
- For the next twelve months we're prioritizing improving the visibility of money and debt management. We're moving away from manual spreadsheets and making urgent fixes to secure our legacy technology estate.

4. Taking a position

Services can be designed to express a position. Organizations that influence economic, societal or environmental conditions can change their services to do this. This might include establishing different rules and criteria, or changing the priorities. Examples:

- We will factor in the true cost to the climate of the carbon emissions from projects we agree to insure, and we will no longer insure projects that don't meet our net zero agenda.
- Instead of an immigration visa that acts as a 'filter', we will enable tech start-ups to go after the best developers and designers in the world from any market.
- Instead of a service culture that treats users with suspicion and operates to minimize support, the service will now do everything possible to help people get the support they need and deserve.

Strategy is design and design is strategy

It often isn't wise, or even possible, to separate 'strategy' from 'design'. Some organizations and services are created according to a mental model of how they should work that combines strategy and design. Others are the result of an unavoidable set of conditions or constraints.

Let's say there's an organization that offers businesses funding for specific activities. These funds could be designed in different ways.

1. Funds could be designed as separate services.

2. The funds could be wrapped together and designed as one service with options to be able to add funding for different activities.

3. Alternatively, each eligible business could be set up to receive funding automatically without having to do anything – a system that takes advantage of whichever options are available for their situation. Users could occasionally add or change options, forget all about it, or disclose that something has changed or that they are no longer eligible.

Sometimes the best approach is one where no one has to do anything for it to just 'happen'. In August 2020, after a series of national lockdowns during the pandemic, the UK government offered a 'eat out to help out' scheme. This gave a 50% discount on food to eat in at an establishment. Rather than ask people to 'apply' for the discount, food establishments signed up to participate and then claimed reimbursement. Whatever the policy intent, this approach at least limited the volume of people that needed to do anything to benefit, as well as reducing the administrative burden of operating the scheme.[7]

Whenever we make choices about how a service works – whether intentionally, unconsciously or because it's assumed that there is only one right way – it has an impact on performance and efficiency. Get to know the default models and concepts in your organization. Raise the assumptions behind them and the constraints that have a limiting effect while also looking for opportunities and allies to help you influence the situation.

Set a delivery approach to optimize confidence

Some organizations don't realize that the chosen approach to a project, portfolio or programme directly affects its success. Our goal is to make this a more considered approach given the context and levels of certainty.

Sometimes the default approach appears to be 'do everything, in parallel, while changing everything about how we work'. This usually entails large transformation programmes alongside multiple project management offices. Folks do their best to track, report and manage all the dependencies, risks and budget while not being granted space for the leadership attention needed to make and reinforce the profound cultural shifts that are required. Work begets work. Attention gets spread too thinly.

You can address these issues by organizing the work and the teams to tackle such problems head on, with the following four ideas.

1. Joining up delivery

If you say 'We need something that brings it all together', many people will nod sagely in agreement – because it's so common for delivery and change in large organizations to be disjointed.

Joining up delivery can start with conjuring sense out of what might feel like chaos to people working internally, and to external users. It doesn't solve the problem of too much low-value work initially, but it can be a step towards highlighting the risks, the gaps and the overlaps to have better conversations about priorities and focus.

If you are involved in a programme of work or a portfolio, chapter 8 provides a way of seeing if work-in-progress maps to outcomes. You can also map all the work across a whole service, or common steps across services, to identify connections and gaps.

If the work is much broader than one service, plot it against what goes on in the life of a user in a given situation: 'everything involved in ageing', for example, or 'buying a house' or 'operating a farm'. Giving external context like this makes it easier for people to see links, dependencies and relationships. If it doesn't fit easily, or if it's hard to do, or if there's a lot of overlapping work tackling the same thing, that's already useful data.

2. Start small but across the whole

Creating a new service means knowing much less at the beginning about what will end up making it a success. Teams that create a part of a service in isolation find it much harder to join up or operate it well as an end-to-end service.

A safer approach can be to identify the absolute minimum needed to start to operate a very basic version of a whole service: a handful of real users or transactions; doing just enough to learn what's actually needed; removing all complexity at this early stage. Avoid the need to scale anything – because that means locking down decisions. But improve it often, to get to a service that works well for larger numbers. Learn what is best to automate, or to do digitally, or whether to invest in supporting it at scale. From a risk perspective, it can be the only way to demonstrate that you absolutely do know what you need to know. It draws out risk that is initially hidden, and it helps teams figure out how much to invest in supporting each part.

By doing this for 10, 50 or 100 users, teams will learn so much, even if a service ultimately needs to support many millions of people. This is about doing everything that is needed, end to end. If teams only build out the first part, they won't learn how to support what comes after, such as compliance, accounting or auditing, or how people get the best outcomes at the other end. Starting small can also reveal and flush out all the activities that aren't needed.

This approach relies on being able to control numbers and timing, and there are different ways to do that, e.g. setting qualification criteria that later expand, making it invite-only, working with limited geographical locations, or time-limiting and segmenting in other ways.

3. Test and learn approach for individual pieces of work
For major portfolios of change in very large organizations, a one-size-fits-all delivery approach doesn't work. It takes ongoing effort from experts to choose the right approach, to help steer and to assess progress.

In these situations you can introduce a 'safer' default: to test, learn and iterate. Start by asking questions such as the following.

- What known problems or opportunities is this solving, and what's our evidence that this is worth it?
- What evidence do we have that we're on the right path?
- What problems could this cause? What are we doing to avoid them?
- What's the biggest risk in terms of building or implementing something that doesn't solve real problems?

To start with, find the one or two teams or projects that would benefit most from a test-and-learn approach. Help them with how to learn about their unknowns, or with what they need in terms of 'digital' expertise and skills that they might not know about. Support them to build and demonstrate value in this way of working.

4. Continuous improvement across the whole
For existing services there's already evidence of what works and what doesn't, but changing the delivery approach is harder because of the complexity of how it's supported. The underlying architecture and supporting capabilities will be more evolved – and potentially constrained – if it's already operating at scale.

If current improvement effort is discontinuous and disjointed, set the ambition to move towards more continuous improvement, at least for the main services, where the opportunity is worthwhile. For large services this realistically involves having a combination of short-, medium- and long-term efforts, making it a more balanced portfolio, e.g. adding small experiments, changes and fixes alongside more significant technology changes.

It's better and healthier for organizations to be able to keep making improvements to deliver greater value, so that services don't reach the point where they need larger, one-off overhaul and modernization – where success is less certain.

Create a strong narrative

Write down the strategy and the organizing principles and priorities, and keep editing them to get to a concise version. Add the implications of what will and won't happen as a result. There can be no room left for doubt or misinterpretation. You don't need to dictate solutions, just state the direction of travel. On that basis it's possible to safely outline what the priorities are likely to be, stretching out some way into the future.

A concise narrative helps everyone to be clear and consistent in what they say to others. It helps to have something to point to, to help people hold the line in the face of pressure to do something different. It's also a good way for leadership to set direction across many teams at once. Examples:

- We'll make the service work for 100 users. Then we'll expand it to 10,000. Then we'll scale it to a million. This means we won't look at scaling technology at all until at least next year.
- We'll learn how to support X, then we'll add support for Y. Only after that will we focus on improving overall efficiency. We won't even look at addressing Z until at least three years from now.

Bad service strategy

What follows are not necessarily bad ideas in themselves, but as a strategy they either aren't very instructive or they actively work against learning.

An 'end state' that hinders learning

Clarity of vision is essential. But some organizations will create a so-called North Star, or vision, that is actually a defined end or ideal state, without connecting it to known problems or risks, or leaving room for learning the ways in which it's wrong.

Establishing what needs to drive the work is not the same as locking down exactly what to build years in advance. The true guiding North Star is what's happening to people outside the organization, and how we can help them be more successful in doing what they need, want or are trying to do. At the heart of this is re-establishing the feedback loop that tells us how to make services perform better. This includes setting out where we are trying to get to – without assuming we know everything up front about how to get there.

It's always important to be scanning the horizon to get a sense of how an industry, a technology or important user needs are likely to change in future. Such stories tell us about possible futures and help us think ahead. But they aren't the tangible strategy and action that set us up to get there, and they don't help us handle the uncertainty that comes with ambitious changes to large, complex services.

An imagined solution

A solution is often set without having, or understanding, a problem that needs solving.

Many organizations wish for a single place or portal where users can access all the services and tools offered: a website, a landing page, a portal or a hub that the organization thinks people will go to.[8] But this is pretty much why we have search engines – at least for services that are publicly accessible. People don't usually need to do everything at once. There is a genuine need for clear content and signposting to help people know about services when and where they need them, but the answer isn't necessarily to build something new or different to provide it.

Similarly, it's common for the larger, older organizations to be working on a new system to 'solve all of the data problems' and 'bring it all together'. Problems with data are a genuine barrier to joined-up services. But the real work to solve them is often to do with addressing culture, ownership, legislation, agreements, formats, standards, unique references and availability. It is not about building a 'data lake'.

'They don't have to like it. They just have to do it.'
Some organizations aim to make a service work better from an inside-out perspective, rather than looking at real-world performance. One example of this is having 'channel shift' as a strategy. This is where organizations prefer customers and users to choose lower-cost or easier-to-support versions of a service: self-serving online rather than calling to speak to someone in person, for example. When budgets are tight, it's important to reduce the operational cost to serve and to be able to offer support where it's needed most. But by adopting a channel-shift approach to meet that goal, it muddies this up with which channel best serves which customers in which situations. Some channels exclude vulnerable people, such as teenagers who can't pay for mobile data, folks travelling abroad, people who are self-isolating, or people who are only able to receive texts rather than phone calls.

The way, rather than the why
Making services more joined up means changing the culture and processes across an organization. That includes moving from one-off projects with fixed outputs and timelines towards more permanent teams and continuous improvement wherever it's valuable to do so. But this is an enabling factor. It sets you up to be in a better position to anticipate and prepare for

inevitable change in the future, and that makes it a wise move. But it doesn't help teams to know what they should do, how or why, and so in and of itself it's not a strategy that directs the actual work.

You often see statements about approaches that sound sensible but that aren't specific to an organization. For example:

- We're transforming the organization
- We're becoming more agile
- We're going to be digital
- We'll be user-centred in everything we do
- We're taking a service design approach
- We're refreshing our technology
- We're going to be data led
- We're modernizing our operations

These things might be entirely necessary. I've certainly said things like this many times. But they don't really say what they mean, which means that people across the organization won't know how to interpret them or apply them to their own area. They therefore aren't a good way of talking about direction.

Separate strategies for enabling teams and functions
Enabling functions such as finance, HR or commercial can sometimes develop their own strategies as if they were separate entities in their own right. A better strategy for these enabling functions could instead be to look at how best to support whatever is needed to make better services – or to do whatever else the organization needs to do to modernize. For example, HR strategy could address how to create the culture and processes required to improve services, or tackle the challenge of hiring, rewarding and growing digital and service specialists. Finance strategy could include making modern iterative development or continuous improvement a prerequisite for funding.

All strategy should move the organization towards better services

If there are already multiple existing strategies for design, customer experience, product, architecture, digital, data and technology, it can make things unclear or even confusing.

It's important to set out what a team or professional practice will do and achieve – and how. This includes the problems it will address to win support for itself, and this is particularly true for human-centred design and modern product development practices, which in older organizations can be absent or not as influential as they should be.

But there's also often no such thing as a design strategy that is entirely separate from a research, service, product or architecture strategy – or, indeed, from any other plans for the customer- and user-facing parts of an organization. There is real value in using professional skills and knowledge to join up and improve the different pieces of work across a service. Rather than having a separate 'architecture' or 'product' strategy, it can be more practical to have a combined 'domain' strategy; one that uses different expertise at different levels to measurably improve services.

Summary

① Set out what a service is there to do, so that you can explore if it does it well enough or not.

② Agree the direction of travel. In broad terms, how do we think services will need to change over time?

③ Organizing principles such as a single imperative or an ambitious measurable goal can help to guide or align work, at least for the next period of time.

④ Consciously choose the delivery approach being taken to max-imize the chances of success, rather than slip into default mode. Point out important options that appear to be overlooked.

⑤ Create a relatable narrative that describes what the strategy means in practice. Make it clear what will and won't happen as a result.

When the strategy is to create a high-performing service at scale

Education & Skills Funding Agency, UK: The Apprenticeship Service

The Education & Skills Funding Agency (ESFA) is accountable for funding education and skills for children, young people and adults. Its flagship apprenticeship service grants funding to employers in the UK to offer apprenticeship positions. It helps apprentices find employers, and helps employers to hire apprentices – and to receive payment.

Eileen Logie is a former deputy director of ESFA and was the original service owner of their flagship apprenticeship service. The challenge from the start was how to scale and develop the structure and process to operate and improve the service con-tinuously. Eileen knew the service would need to grow rapidly to meet developing policy needs and employer demand, as she explains below.[9]

> Scaling up was critical. Creating a good service and building in scale was the strategy. We wanted to make 3 million apprentice-ships available, so working with the organizations to provide them was critical. There are 1.5 million employers in the UK and we needed to be able to support them all. Knowing the need to scale drove some of our early choices about how to structure and store data, what platforms to use, what tools to use for market-ing or support models, as well as how to describe value in the

investment cases that sat behind these decisions. We had to put tooling in to help tell us when we have a problem across the service, or where people are getting stuck, how far they're getting through it, where content could be improved, or if the underlying code is wrong. We needed to understand the scale of any issues – if there's a pattern or if it's just individual cases.

We had user researchers to help us understand the 'why' – what's causing the problems and what we need to do to fix it. Because of the scale, we had to manage failure demand carefully, with a process to identify problems, triage them and then prioritize. It meant circling back to the build teams to learn from it, when questions from customers got asked more than once, or where we released code with issues.

Customer numbers have increased tenfold through the service, so our strategy of focusing on scaling our support models and on our ability to iterate and improve performance really paid off.

Starting small – a live service to learn from
Department for Work & Pensions (DWP), UK: Universal Credit
Universal Credit is the UK government's flagship support service to help people with living costs and to find work. It was developed as a new, in-house digital service after a major reset in 2013. The approach was to start small, to learn what was going to be needed and where, in order to operate it well at scale. The leadership initially prioritized making the experience for customers as simple as possible, by manually handling behind-the-scenes operational processes.

Deb Boore, transformation and delivery director, Universal Credit, DWP, explains.[10]

We decided that while the service was small, we could cope with the tools for DWP users not being fully developed, as long as the customer experience was good. We knew we'd have a job on our hands to make it better for colleagues, but if we didn't do it this way, we'd have no customer feedback to improve from and might have made the wrong design decisions for everyone. It's so important to learn first before deciding where to build in scale or automate processes. It was the right decision, but people initially thought we didn't care about operations, when the opposite was true. The majority of our users are DWP customers or claimants, and that needs to be a good experience even if it is not used every day. Our colleagues use it all day, every day, so it had to work really well for them too. And that meant learning what was really needed by operating it first with very small numbers.

We wanted to test with real users and live data as early as possible. Not just a theoretical 'model office' that wouldn't tell us the real problems and scenarios. We set up a mini telephony service centre in the corner of the floor upstairs from the Jobcentre. We brought all the product functions together on-site and we tracked each individual customer through the process. And we had user researchers downstairs in the Jobcentre talking to our customers. With this approach we were able to test very early versions of the service and understand what needed to be in place, to deliver the right outcomes and a good user experience, before we expanded to more customers and added more colleagues to the service.

Chapter 7

Position teams around services

Map the service together. Build roadmaps together. Do user research together. Choose options together. Working with each other can be hard and messy. People are different. But it's still worth it to do it together.

It's not unusual to have dozens – or even hundreds – of teams working on services, on pieces of work that affect services, or as part of separate functions that influence how well services can work. But what is 'a team' if working across whole services requires the combined expertise of operations, user researchers, product managers, developers, designers, policy and strategy, not to mention legal, commercial, procurement, finance, fraud and compliance?

It's not as if one person or a single team could redesign a service that involves frontline and behind-the-scenes operations and contact centres, that is supported by technology and delivered across many channels: in person, by phone, through an app, a website and online forums. It takes blended teams, working together. But how do we organize so that the people that need to work together do so (and can still meet and find out about each other serendipitously), while also identifying and maintaining the healthy boundaries and focus that teams need to get stuff done. Let's look at the different kinds of teams that large services need.

The types of teams you need

In their book *Team Topologies*, Matthew Skelton and Manuel Païs identify four team types for building and running software-enriched services: stream aligned, enabling, complicated subsystem and platform teams.[1]

With their permission I've drawn on this same structure and expanded it to reflect the reality of large end-to-end services. I add two further team types to include the variety of operational activities and the need for coordination when significant changes are happening in a complex domain (ahead of settling on a direction and rhythm of working that supports this more organically).

1. *Service teams* deliver valuable changes for users, operations and organization outcomes. Some organizations will call these product, delivery or digital teams.

2. *Depth teams* research and resolve complex issues and topics or undertake specialist analysis or development on behalf of other teams.

3. *Common-capability teams* develop and iterate supporting capabilities: the internal products, tools or processes that services need, as well as ways to make the other teams faster, safer or better.

4. *Enabling teams* do everything else that's needed to support, assist, defend and unblock all the other teams and individual disciplines.

5. *Coordinating teams* help direct, connect and communicate when there is a lot of activity across a service or multiple services. They develop strategy, figure out delivery approaches in a complex landscape, or coordinate a response when significant events take place. They can also be involved in assessing and constructively challenging work.

6. *Operational teams* deliver, operate and improve services and important capabilities on an ongoing basis. This includes user-facing frontline and behind-the-scenes activity, customer support and contact handling, and other specialized teams involved in service provision.

What the different types of team do

Service teams

These teams are at the centre of important changes for users, for the organization and for operations. They work directly to create or improve a service or a major stage of it, or on a piece of work that could affect service performance. Service teams are in a position to have the greatest influence on solving issues and addressing the major opportunities to improve. They focus on the following areas.

- Valuable change for customers and users. What will help them be more successful at what they need to do or achieve?
- Changing how a service is operated. This could include how well we support internal users, or how well we use technology to handle routine tasks. Additionally, they try to make it more sustainable in terms of cost to serve.
- Changes to improve service outcomes, demand, success rates, uptake or compliance.

Service teams shouldn't be restricted to using technology, design, process, data or infrastructure as the only means to achieve changes, but should look at all aspects that realistically play a role. Examples include how policy is operationalized, how simple the rules are, an organization's cultural beliefs and ways of working, and everything else that affects how well something works in real life. Services can grow to have dozens of teams working on different stages or at different levels.

When folks talk about multidisciplinary teams in the agile sense, they can overlook the truly multidisciplinary nature of whole services and the need for teams that reflect this. A service team might include the following.

- People with current or very recent experience of operating or providing a service, including frontline, contact centre and other operational staff.
- People focused on strategy or policy – and 'making it real'.
- Specialist practitioners with the skills to help their team(s) learn, test, deliver change and iterate from there. These individuals are closest to what some people call an agile, digital or product team: product managers, user researchers, developers, technical leads, designers, content designers, business analysts, delivery managers and testers.
- People with experience of specialist areas, such as commercial, procurement, compliance, fraud and error, legal or regulation.
- People who are good at communicating and telling the story inwards and upwards.

This shift to true multidisciplinary teams is now happening more widely in both the public and private sectors, including in modern technology companies. This means hiring practices need to increasingly identify candidates who naturally think about other perspectives, not just their own specialism.

Depth teams

Depth teams form to explore complex issues when specific problems arise. They can provide additional support, often temporarily, to prevent service teams being distracted from the day-to-day work that delivers the most value. The make-up of these teams depends on the type of issue and where the biggest risk is: whether it's more to do with users, technology, data, policy or something else. Wherever possible, this work should remain within service teams to keep the knowledge with them. However, here are a few examples where it could make sense for an additional team to add expertise or bring focus.

- Investigating a legacy IT system challenge to ascertain if it's likely to be worth attempting to integrate what already exists with what's being developed for a new service, or whether the constraints of doing so would hamper any improvement.
- Doing some research and development to explore the potential for technology to solve a difficult data challenge, requiring niche skill sets to figure out what's possible, what the right approach involves, or the ethical implications or risks.
- A people or design challenge that hasn't been well solved, such as how to develop graphs or maps in a way that's inclusive of people in realistic situations with realistic capabilities, rather than it being deemed acceptable that only some people are able to make sense of or use data.
- A policy challenge such as further research, analysis or evidence-gathering to collate facts or to detail and weigh up the differences between options.

The creation of policy labs and policy design teams in parts of the UK government is one example of depth teams. These tend to be protected teams, with space to test and learn, alongside people from operations and policy. They work away from day-to-day operations to try to find answers to problems or to identify opportunities.

Common-capability teams

These teams support other teams by developing, procuring and supporting products, tools and processes that other teams can use to do common activities better, faster or with less risk. As such, their customers and users are internal teams, but always in pursuit of supporting overall service performance.

The need for these teams stems from scale. It's not where you start. Common-capability teams develop or make available *what was already needed and developed* by service teams themselves. But separating them out saves these teams from doing the same work over and over, meaning a standard can be established or maintained. Separation can also nurture and protect the domain knowledge needed to develop or procure specific capabilities.

Below are some examples of common capabilities.

- Developing or making available the tools, products and platforms needed by the service and used by service teams. Examples include the GOV.UK Design System,[2] platforms like GOV.UK Pay[3] and Notify,[4] and capabilities to support identity verification or authorization.
- Tools and processes that help a team to learn, build and deploy changes more quickly.

There is significant risk in separating out teams to work on common capabilities and components away from service teams.[5] It's a risk that's often downplayed, and hidden from leadership. Centralizing critical decisions removes them from the reality of what service teams are learning and how services need to be iterated. The choices made can place huge constraints on the ability of service teams to learn and take the right actions. Common teams need to be really clear on goals and spend time with their users, adjusting their view of what it is that they are building. The minute teams are unhelpfully constrained for important parts of a service, they won't be learning and they won't be able to respond to what the organization needs them to do.

For new or radically changing services, common teams should never be established from the start. Wait for the need to reveal itself once service teams have tried, tested and proved the need for common elements by building or using versions themselves that can be spun off and expanded.

Enabling teams

Enabling teams are the people, functions and business services that sit around or outside of services to support them, by developing and maintaining standards, dealing with barriers and blockers, and protecting wider corporate, policy or user-related interests. They often include skills and experience that could, or should, be embedded within service teams. But sometimes the need is ad hoc, or there's greater value in centralizing support. For this reason, enabling teams vary, but they usually include

- finance;
- procurement;
- legal and legislative or regulatory compliance;
- professional support, which might include guidance, standards and controls to assure the work of individual professions, as well as people who make available knowledge, equipment and processes that are needed by specialist professions to support their work across service teams;
- HR – and often support for hiring, procuring and supplier management for specialist individuals and suppliers, as well as changes to culture;
- policy specialists;
- experts in modern delivery, technology and design, who develop guidance and standards and provide support to help other teams learn, test and iterate; who offer consultative services on good practice or on what's needed; who provide specialist skills and advice, along with other recommendations, to ensure investment; and who support the development of some of these capabilities in others; and
- communications.

These teams function best when they work in the spirit of doing everything possible to support other teams delivering actual change and, thereby, value. Enabling teams work to reduce the cognitive load of other teams or individuals and to unblock problems, maintain or improve standards. They don't exist to simply repeat company policy or control all service design decisions.

It's much more effective to embed individuals from these enabling functions within the core service team(s) if the nature of the work in a service or depth team heavily involves one of these areas. An HR or comms person who is working directly with, or across, service teams and is invested in making it a success – as opposed to a business management partner working from afar – can be invaluable. The performance of an enabling team isn't about the rigour with which it upholds corporate process. It's about how simple and fast it is to give service teams (and other teams that are delivering value) what is needed, how long it takes, and how much back-and-forth there is. It's a shift in culture: away from a function being considered solely as the protector of corporate risk, and instead becoming a supporting capability and an enabler of how well services – and teams – perform.

There are other enabling activities beyond the usual corporate functions that a large organization needs for better-performing services at scale, including those in the following list.

- Creating and sharing insight and guidance to keep other teams productive, prevent duplication or maintain good standards. This could include translators and knowledge management: people who can ensure teams continue to know what they need to know, and who can set up new teams with the right context, avoiding unhelpful duplication of effort. For example: universally applicable lists of users and user needs; good practice for technology and data; guidance for how to handle specific types of data.

- Operationalizing and scaling what individual professions need as they grow: consent handling for researchers, for instance, and codes of practice.
- Support to help embed the conditions for modern ways of working, and to establish and protect newer 'digital', technology, data and human-centred design skill sets and professions in more traditional organizations.

Coordinating teams

With the right structure and support, many teams are able to self-organize and coordinate and don't need a whole other team to do this for them. But in very large organizations and for complex services undergoing significant change, it can require people with more time available to coordinate effort and direction across the whole, at least for a while before service teams and leadership settle on effective ways of working themselves.

These teams tend to be made up of lead professions and individual leaders. There's a careful balance to strike. In some organizations the presence of coordinating teams can be an 'anti-pattern' that suggests service teams aren't otherwise aligned, well structured, supported or able to work to outcomes. Coordinating teams should aim to step back as quickly as possible, or refocus on anticipating issues and removing blockers. Chapter 9 includes more details of service leadership and coordinating activity.

Operational teams

The operation of large services can include dozens, hundreds or even thousands of people – working on the front line or in contact centres, carrying out tasks behind the scenes, in transport and logistics, or delivering expert professional services. These are often known as 'operational' teams, although separating the function of operations away from other functions – digital and technology, say, or user-centred design or policy – is often a barrier to joining up services and improving their performance.

In traditional organizations you might hear the phrase 'build, run, operate', with the suggestion that different teams are involved at each phase. But in modern tech companies, the principle is to reduce such handoffs between teams. Werner Vogels[6] (chief technology officer and vice president at Amazon) coined the phrase 'you build it you run it' to mean that the teams that create the technology should – where it makes sense to – also operate, support and continuously improve it rather than handing that part over to another team. This could be a good principle to apply for service teams and common-capability teams where they are building technology that's important to services, instead of asking a different 'IT team' to 'run' or 'maintain' something once it's built.

But that's different to the operational teams I'm talking about here, which specialize in delivering and supporting parts of a wider service. Roles vary but some common ones include

- frontline staff,
- caseworkers or case managers,
- client relationship managers,
- contact centre staff,
- quality improvement and assurance teams,
- compliance officers and
- team leaders.

The trick is to organize activity in a way that reduces or prevents the handoff culture, so that operational teams can do what's needed to solve problems first time around. This includes structuring things in such a way that those operational teams don't get stuck using unhelpful tools and technology, processes and procedures designed by others from a distance, that don't work well – and that they can't iterate or adapt to what they learn, to the situation, or to local context.

John Seddon shares many examples for addressing avoidable demand for services by shifting from leadership 'command and control' to organizing to best deliver value to customers and communities.[7]

How to operate services well is a subject that could fill several further books, but I want to share three important aspects that Philippa Elworthy (DWP) introduced me to that help to reduce handoffs and improve overall performance. These are

1. how we design and support ongoing training and communications for operational teams;

2. putting in place mechanisms so that operational teams work closely together with other teams who build and change parts of services; and

3. championing these practices and taking the steps needed to make them a reality, not just 'talking the talk'.

Chapter 8 includes practical advice for how to make these changes, with examples of organizations who do this well.

Don't start with every team

If you're starting work on a new service, or you're at the beginning of radically changing an existing service, don't set up all these teams at once. Grow from one service team if you possibly can, to learn what's really needed, while allowing healthy working practices to settle. Evolve outwards from there.

In particular, don't establish a common capabilities team from the start. It's far safer to evolve what is common from individual teams working on services than it is to try to predict up front what and how to do this. If a common-capability team already exists and it's working at distance from the teams working on services, then it can be safer to stop or restructure.

Of course, the make-up of teams and the number of them will vary depending on the size of the organization, on its services, on the scale of any change and on budgets. In the organization you work with, teams might not go by these names. They might not work in the way described here. There could be just five people or five teams instead of five dozen. Regardless, our goal is to establish the conditions for more teams to be doing better work, more cohesively, improving services in every possible way.

Learn how to make better services together

Wright's law[8] says that we get faster at building technology as time goes by – not because of scale, but because each time we perform a task we learn how to do it better. A similar principle applies to teams working on services. We don't know initially how best to work together across so many disciplines and moving parts. It takes time to figure that out, and it becomes more efficient over time.

In emergency care, simulations are used as a core part of teaching practice, but really they're about teamwork more than testing any one individual's clinical skills: learning how to listen and communicate as a collective to get the best outcomes for the patient. In contrast, the way in which some teams operate in large organizations makes it seem as if they can see neither the end user of the service nor the other people working with them; their focus is on their own ability to fix the lighting, move the bed or apply a bandage.

This is one reason why many organizations move to permanent multidisciplinary service teams, not one-off projects involving people who don't know one another. As we've seen during the pandemic, services with permanent service teams in place were in a much stronger position to handle the sudden change in priorities.[9]

Working as a whole can go against the grain for some people who consider going it alone to be easier. Working with others can be hard and messy. But doing things together is still worth it.

Setting out some organizing principles can help reinforce the need for this, as well as providing a benchmark to review against if things aren't working so well. It's a good exercise for a team to develop their own when they form. Here are a few example principles to seed the right actions.

- The whole team delivers the whole. This means hands-on design and delivery, rather than consulting, reviewing or checking. No hand-offs, except when it absolutely makes sense in the context.
- Emphasize creating and implementing, rather than just thinking or planning. Actual change is how you measure and deliver value – or learn what will be valuable.
- Genuinely care about the whole, with people who are able to look beyond their individual role.
- Everyone must be willing to challenge the established thinking and work together to do so. Leadership also needs to be open to changes to working practice – otherwise things stay the same.

Summary

① Shift from functional teams with hand-offs to whole teams delivering, or joining up, whole services.

② There are six team types involved in delivery of whole services: service teams, depth teams, common-capability teams, enabling teams, coordinating teams and operational teams.

③ Learning how to work together is as important as figuring out the right way to design and run services. Develop principles to set expectations.

Establishing strong teams and capabilities to build from

NHS England, UK

When organizations have established more permanent multidisciplinary teams they are better positioned to respond to change and opportunities. By staying together over longer periods, it can allow teams to develop the building blocks and ways of working that make them more efficient. The recent Covid-19 pandemic resulted in many organizations needing to develop new services within days or weeks, rather than months or years.

NHS England supports NHS staff at work, helps people get the best care, and uses the nation's health data to drive research and transform services.

Tero Väänänen is head of design at NHS England. He explains how prior effort and investment in teams and capabilities meant they were already working at pace before the pandemic hit.[10]

To some extent, the rapid response to the pandemic would not have been as successful had we not already had some of the building blocks in place from years of investment.

We already had mature public-facing products, digital services and platforms in place; the NHS website had been redesigned in 2018, the NHS App and NHS Login launched the same year, to mention a few. They had been designed and built using user-centred and iterative agile methods, and had already gained reliability and a solid user base, and thus provided an excellent platform to rapidly build COVID-19 services on.

Whilst redesigning the NHS website, we had started to establish our design system, design principles and the NHS design standard in the NHS Service Manual, providing tried-and-tested components, guidance and standards to use to design and build usable and accessible digital services at pace. The prototyping kit accompanying the design system supports rapid iterative design and user research, whilst the design system provides production-ready code for anyone to use.

We also had multidisciplinary teams already in place working in an agile, user-centred way. We were able to shape the problems with the teams who already knew how to work effectively together to solve a problem. This is in contrast to forming a new team, which often means longer time for the teams to establish how to work well together. In reality, we did both; we simply did not have enough teams ready to tackle every problem the pandemic threw our way.

Going into the pandemic in the beginning of 2020 and starting to build the response to this would not have been as quick nor successful if we had not made the investment years ahead to build up these foundations. It still wasn't easy, but to know we had the teams who had the right processes and standards to rely on, the reliable products, digital services and platforms to build on, definitely made it more successful.

Caring about what others care about
Retailers

How well multidisciplinary teams are able to work together across services reflects the culture of the organization. Do people want to collaborate – and are they able to? Do teams have the same shared value of the right thing to do for their customers and their colleagues?

One professional who has worked with major retailers and brands shared the following insight.

It's all connected: colleagues' experience in the warehouse, how stores know what to buy and how they pick suppliers, getting products into store, how products might be picked by an online delivery team, to a delivery van and a driver, to the website or checkout experience and how we communicate throughout – a journey doesn't start and end on the website.

To provide a good experience or a good service at the scale of the biggest retailers, you need to work with people you haven't worked with before – where you don't know what their skill sets are.

But when you have a common mission, which means you all care, and you get excited about what you can do together with your specific experience and expertise – whether that's 'we care about making a nice product', or 'we care about running a great store', or 'we care that customers are happy' – it's bringing everyone around a vision. And it requires that people learn from each other and are willing to trust what others can bring to the mission. It's really interesting to learn what the folks in the risk team do, for example, what they care about, and from a digital perspective why we may have to consider something we've never really thought about before. If you're a good colleague and care about customers, you should really want to do that. It comes down to your approach and how you think about things, how open minded or curious you might be. You can't be closed off to what others care about.

Chapter 8

Create plans that change as you learn more about reality

The goal is to move the conversation from 'what do we get and when' to 'what do we need to do and learn (by when)'.

Planning helps to create and communicate the conditions that generate better services. But if someone has already created a very detailed plan for a service or programme – stretching out over months or years – that doesn't match the reality of what's safe to predict, it limits the ability to learn what needs to be learned – and to act on it. Goals change, we learn new things, there will be unexpected events.

Our goal is to help our organizations learn what they need to learn quickly, safely and with greater efficacy – and to be able to adapt. This means that plans need to be able to change in response to real data from exposure to users and operations.

All that said, it's a significant undertaking to fundamentally change how complex services work. Careful consideration is needed in order to figure out the implications of changing how something works, through the different layers that build up over time. But for some organizations, rather than a plan that supports learning, a detailed long-term plan is taken to be a reassurance and a 100% commitment to what's on it– even if that reassurance is false. Such a plan can even come to be seen as more valuable than doing the actual work. Or it can be a requirement of obtaining funding in the first place.

The problem, then, is when detailed plans result in unrealistic expectations, promises and 'targets'. They're nothing more than predictions that require people to riskily decide the answers up front and then stick to them, even when situations aren't well understood.

For events that haven't occurred or don't exist yet – events for which there's no evidence or real data – an upfront detailed plan should be a shared concern, especially if it's been drawn up by people who aren't deeply aware of operations or users or by people without relevant recent experience.

This might work for predictable situations. Establishing a new supermarket branch that is a clone of another is a repeatable pattern, as is a factory that churns out standardized components. But that's very different to creating or changing the complex service environments that this book is about. There, we only learn what really works, or what the risks actually are, the closer we get to reality.

This chapter looks at how to handle planning for complex services where discovering new problems or making hard decisions and trade-offs happens every day.

Create simpler plans

Even if you know what you're aiming for, how to make it a reality in your particular organization or industry, or for your users, in their specific situations, has to be learned and iterated. We cannot know all we need to know in advance.

It is possible to manage the risk of getting it wrong. For plans to be credible they simply need a suitable and accurate level of detail. Setting parameters, rather than creating very detailed plans, is a better way of guiding teams to learn what's needed. For many organizations this is a profound change. It requires trust and healthy two-way communication. But it can also start to threaten power structures.

You can make a start by creating a shockingly simple – and probably wrong – plan: a horizontal timeline, without dates to start with, and with just five to ten activities and a few important events on it. Work backwards from somewhere you think you will need to be by a certain point in time for it to be credible, and then add further details as you know more.

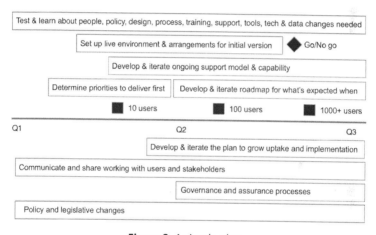

Figure 8. A simple plan.

This will concern people who want a detailed plan, and it will worry people who don't think enough is known to have any plan. But really it's just the start of a 'more right' plan. It's much easier to know what is needed, what the implications are or what the next priority is once something is working in a basic way than it is if you don't start at all.

Some people will ask for details up front that can't possibly be known before steps are taken on a smaller scale. They might ask for exact costs, for example, or for volumes, or certainty on dates or features. But we can often triangulate using what we do know, and do just enough research to gather some initial evidence, and then assess that along with the severity of the risk of getting it wrong. It's usually possible to know at least a little more, quickly. As long as we can easily change course, it matters less if we're wrong. By setting out in one direction, regardless of how little is known, you could be able to gather the evidence you need – or the real answers – faster.

This plan is not the same as a service roadmap, which is usually about the design and build of the service itself (or a component part that affects services). Instead, it describes all the accompanying activity that supports the service being developed in a large organization, such as important problems to learn about or solve; major decision points; governance, training and awareness; expected iteration of the service; adoption plans; and communication. Set this out in the right way and it can create the space needed for learning and iteration towards better-performing services.

This (sometimes profound) change in approach takes time to feel comfortable with. People need to see it working to trust that it's different and yet works. Iterate the plan weekly or daily – or whatever reflects the rhythm that teams are working to. It will become more detailed, and more right, as you go.

As an alternative to creating a simple timeline, you can also write a few simple statements about what it is that's going to have happened in six or twelve months' time that will help to communicate confidently and clearly to leadership or stakeholders. They should be basic, but specific.

In six months' time we will have a very limited but live end-to-end service that is operated manually for up to 100 users that we will be testing and learning from. In twelve months' time we will have added tools to better support operational decision making, and we expect to have scaled the service to support up to 5,000 users.

In three months' time we will have learned and established a process to train and update all of our contact centre and frontline teams, to allow us to change and improve the service continuously, while prioritizing critical support improvements. In nine months' time we will have scaled the number of options available for users, and they will be able to apply online.

Some teams use this format to create an imaginary press release or a short delivery note for a board.

Embed an approach that de-risks service delivery

Modern organizations create the conditions necessary for teams to learn how best to deliver desired outcomes, rather than churn out predetermined outputs that could easily miss important goals.

'Users successfully and confidently do what they came to do' could be a desired outcome. 'Grow to support 20,000 users doing X' is a goal (or a target). 'Launch an app, a website or a database' is an output. And 'what it will take to make something that ends up with 20,000 users successfully doing the right thing' is what we need to learn.

What it takes to achieve outcomes is not obvious. For this reason, people can feel reluctant to bet their career, their reputation or their bonus – or simply carry the delivery risk – on something that doesn't sound certain, even if this situation reflects reality.

To move people towards outcomes while staying on what can feel like firmer ground, try breaking the work into

- what we know or believe needs to happen,
- what we need to learn, and
- how we'll do this.

This nuance makes it an easier conversation to have, especially within a cultural context that weds an organization to very detailed plans. This can reassure people who feel uncomfortable while still grounding activities and choices in what we have evidence for and where we need more. There needn't be a binary choice between an 'outputs and milestones' plan and an 'outcomes' plan.

Build consensus about the priority risks to address

Having detailed plans, risk registers (i.e. lists of possible risks), boards and authorities are some of the ways in which large organizations address risk. But programmes of work can become so large and complicated that people get caught up in planning, meetings and endless reporting of risk. These processes can even become more meaningful to some than the actual outcomes of the work – and without handling one of the biggest risks of all: failing to create something 'useful, usable and actually used' – a phrase coined by the Society for Innovation, Technology and Modernisation[1] and highlighted by the forms specialist and author Caroline Jarrett.[2]

By identifying what's most likely to be difficult or very uncertain early on, teams can tackle major problems more quickly than they would with a sequential plan. For example, you might be some months down the line before discovering that the data the project relied on was never going to be available.

Here are some examples of what could be significant risks.

- The risk that a proposition won't be attractive enough to encourage at least 10,000 people to sign up to it and commit to taking action.
- The risk that we are unable to access data held in a legacy system without spending unreasonable effort.
- The risk that we'll be unable to communicate a complex proposition in a way our audience will understand.
- The risk that we will be unable to arrange for the legal teams of six different organizations to enter data-sharing agreements that a new service will rely on to be able to operate.

- The risk that it will be impossible to check compliance remotely, without having to send someone to a physical location in person each time.
- The risk that we'll be unable to do what's needed within a fixed budget or at a cost that is sustainable.

The goal of this exercise isn't to try to demonstrate all the ways in which a project can be hard, risky or flawed. It's to help deliver something valuable in reality. Map out important 'facts' across a service that would need to be true but that aren't well known or evidenced today. Explore what people are already worried about, what could cause real problems, or where there's evidence that something significant won't work. See where you can agree on what is critical, as well as where you are least certain.

What we need to learn about first

Start a profound shift in culture by adjusting the focus to 'what we need to learn', not just 'what tools or features do we get'. You could use the structure in chapter 2 to map out what's important to learn or improve on at each stage of a service, whether that's through a temporary prototype or from the first introduction of a live service.

Rather than just delivering a 'technical proof of concept', for example, what we actually need to learn could include the following.

- How best can we support necessary changes to process and ways of working? And what are the barriers we'll need to address?
- What communications to internal users and partners are likely to be needed? What are the right methods, timelines and frequencies?

- What capabilities and activity will we, or others, need in order to support a significant change? Who will we need, where, and doing what?
- Could any part of what we're proposing worsen performance by increasing the time a critical task takes?
- How important is it to be able to do X first rather than Y? What's the impact of doing (any of) it later?

Unless it's already obvious, often we are only able to learn what the true priority is by making a start, somewhere. Since it's only the first activity in what is likely a lot of work ahead, it needs to happen quickly.

Here are a few examples of ways to learn rapidly, by taking a first step.

- Prototyping and testing with users to reach a design where most people who try it can do what they came to do.
- Setting different pricing and incentive levels to see at what amount it is persuasive.
- Mapping compliance issues end to end with a domain specialist, and identifying what needs to change to be able to enforce a particular idea.
- Setting up a very basic version of a service, as end to end as possible, and running it manually with very low numbers of users (or transactions) to learn what's needed, what's a problem and what the next priority is.
- Asking a technical lead to spend five days exploring the likely complexity of an option that relies on integrating with a legacy IT system.
- Finding out how to back away from an initial 'good enough' tech choice once it has served its initial purpose.
- Creating two versions of something to see which is best.

There are excellent guides that go into more detail on how to do all this.[3]

Not a 'backlog' but a list to draw from

It's common among teams that are delivering pieces of work that affect or change a service to refer to a *backlog*. This word can send the wrong message to some people in whose professional world a backlog is a pile of cases that you have to work through in turn in order to progress. If people believe we already know up front all the work that is needed in this way, it will feel odd to avoid plotting it all on a timeline or Gantt chart. It can help, therefore, to clarify that a backlog isn't a to-do list but a list of potential work for a team to take on. Each time you review it, you have the opportunity to figure out what's most important. And by doing work and seeing what works in reality, you'll be in a much better position to know what other work is most important next.

Planning across different pieces of work

Often there isn't a clear, linear path towards a goal. Some teams will set out what is being worked on now, what's next, and what's in the future. The 'now, next, future' roadmap, coined by Janna Bastow (CEO and co-founder of ProdPad and co-founder of Mind the Product),[4] gives a moment-in-time view and an idea of the future without committing to a sequential order or doing it all at once. John Cutler (product evangelist and coach) refers to this as a 'suitably detailed' roadmap.[5]

It's a neat way of separating out

- what we can, should – and therefore are – doing or achieving now;
- what's likely to be next; and
- what's possible in future, the priority of which we can determine later.

It's wise to include a fourth category of 'what we won't be doing' to reduce ambiguity.

Keep the link with whole services or a wider theme

Make sure that plans include a reference to the service(s) to keep the work in context. You can try grouping common themes of work by colour, shape and label across a plan to track it collectively.

For example, some teams group all the work in progress in terms of

- how it addresses a particular domain or problem across a larger portfolio, e.g. 'debt collection';
- which organization 'mission' it represents, e.g. 'make it a great place to work', or 'make services that are more human-centred';
- coordinating effort around a particular set of user needs, such as 'assisted digital' support, or 'reduce the time taken to get a definitive answer to users'.

Jeff Patton's book *User Story Mapping* provides a useful model for how to make the link between the work that is underway and the user journey that that work is intended to support.[6]

What to do if a plan is already agreed

Many organizations are conditioned to working with very detailed long-term plans, while others 'roll out' off-the-shelf technology suddenly, without much consideration to the support available, to the change involved, to communications or training or interaction with all the people involved in a service.

Lots of people still manage to make good things happen to services anyway. If a very detailed but unhelpful plan is already in circulation, whether it's for a service or an entire organization, there are a few things you can try to change the situation.

Don't wait for permission

Go ahead and create a massively simplified and clearer plan or view – even if there's already a more complex one being used. Start to use it alongside – and eventually instead of – the existing plan.

This simpler view is immediately helpful because it's easier to read and understand, so more people will have the chance to engage with the work and provide scrutiny that's useful, more often. You can position it as complementary:

> We do have a more detailed plan, but the detail isn't yet based on data or evidence, because we're not there yet. So in the meantime here's a simpler view, which is based on what we currently know to be the reality, to help us get on top of the situation now and manage expectations, to avoid backtracking later. We're structuring teams to learn quickly about what's most difficult, and to build detail around what is more certain.

Over time it is possible to demonstrate to others the validity of working with more realistic and adaptable plans in this way. But it's a major cultural shift that often won't happen without people experiencing that it is possible – and without some openness and protection from leadership to be able to do things differently.

Set out the logic

Rather than spend time arguing about what's in scope or out of scope, or when some part of a plan should be delivered, instead set out a tight story about what you're doing – backed by very clear logic. This logic should directly answer the risks. It should cover the following.

> We want to achieve X. We believe we'll achieve that by doing Y. If we're successful we'll see an increase in A, a decrease in B or a neutral effect on C.
>
> This is complex territory, there are unknowns and risks. So we're taking a test-and-learn approach to ground what we're doing in evidence from reality.*
>
> To make sure this effort is valuable, we're prioritizing the critical things to learn and we're taking rapid action to get the answers we need to assure the approach.
>
> Right now that means we're getting evidence for approach G over approach H. We've timeboxed this effort so that by [date] we'll be clearer what it will take and what the result is likely to be.

The governance process described in chapter 11 can help support and assure progress. If anyone disagrees, doubts the logic or wants to change the approach, they also need to be able to provide an alternative story that's compelling, and they need to be accountable for the risks or propose how to manage them in another way.

Constructively challenge the constraints

We don't always have free rein to decide exactly how to design, set up or operate services. In a large organization with many existing parts, it's a balance between using what's already in place and taking the opportunity to create what will work well for a specific context. Some professions work across the organization to seek to reduce duplication of capabilities and effort across services. But sometimes it just sounds like duplication until you understand the context.

---

* Even so-called off-the-shelf implementations of technology in complex service environments often still require significant process changes, training and communication, if not extensive customization, localization and ongoing maintenance.

Understanding and weighing up the reality of the impact of these choices is critical. To be realistic and responsible, we can't accept any and all constraints from people, who could be acting on old or wrong information or assumptions, without some form of due diligence. For example, the practice of separating out contact centres, back office and shared services might have been a view of best practice once upon a time, but when feedback loops are tighter and the wrong sentence on a website immediately drives demand to the contact centre, services need different models that can react faster.

On the other hand, many product managers end up regretting the work put in to develop a unique product and set of rules for just one team or one client when they realize how it might have been developed in a way that could neatly support many more teams, customers and services.

We need to know

- how we'll know the cost or impact of constraints for our particular service or situation;
- how much we'll be able to learn about the context, rather than just learning about the constraints; and
- what we'd look to as the evidence base if we need to challenge the constraints – or analyse how valid they are.

If there are hard constraints on choices that will result in serious restrictions on services, make sure a plan is being considered for how to move on from that position in the future. Flag the important questions, and what we'll need to learn about them, when we are able to do so – and add this to the plan.

Resist pressure to fake a plan

If you are under pressure to build an overly detailed plan, first map out the important questions: the unknowns, what will make this hard, and what is most risky. Do this as a group to build consensus about what you genuinely know and what isn't known yet.

Use this view to constructively challenge the certainty expected, especially if there isn't a concrete plan to do the work to learn more before committing. Engage with risk management professionals and individual members of governance forums who can be allies in this situation.

Some risk-management and portfolio-management teams can be backed into a corner themselves, becoming an administrative and reporting function instead of genuinely addressing risk. If this is the situation, find the individuals who recognize it as such and work with them to change it. Reconstruct a more realistic plan together. If there are hard commitments that are genuinely immovable, timebox the work to learn, in order to assess the level of risk being carried when we get to each point. The assessment process outlined in chapter 10 will help to track whether we're improving the risk situation over time or continuing with the same levels.

Work around upfront projections

Boards and directors have a legal duty to know whether funds are being spent wisely and safely. Teams involved in financial planning, analysis and tracking of spend have often already modelled how money will be spent on services (or on work that affects them) into the future. In some situations this presents a barrier to being able to change a plan, and it doesn't sit well with the approach of learning and iterating as we go.

It's helpful to share with colleagues what we are more certain about, and explain what we aren't sure of, why that is, and what we can do to become more certain. Professionals experienced in how to model and project into the future can factor what we do know with some certainty into their modelling. Where we don't know any better than what is already in a model, then keep to what is there, stating the caveats clearly. Ideally, use ranges rather than fixed numbers, and show different scenarios to emphasize the issue with certainty given the stage of the work.

The problem with target operating models

For many, a 'target' operating model (TOM) provides some clarity about where an organization, function or service is heading. But for a very complex organization or service, a team could easily spend six months just creating a proposed TOM before any actual work begins, by which time everything will have changed.

Another issue is that a TOM is often set as a model to aim for without saying what it is that people are trying to solve about the current structure, and without discussing how they will know whether it will work better – or what the implications are.

It's usually unclear to everyone involved what an operating model even means – even the people who make them. For some, it means 'everything about how an organization works'. Rather than talk about operating models, I now think about specifics such as the flow of work, what 'success' looks like, the activities needed, what else is needed, who and where. This might include the capabilities, the people and teams, the processes and ways of working, and the supporting infrastructure. And most importantly, work out what is actually needed by making it clear these are questions to learn the answers to, not rectangles to be pre-filled on a diagram. When I refer to operating models here I focus on what's needed to deliver services for people outside the organization, without directly addressing everything else that large organizations need to operate normally (including tax, accounting, payroll, insurance, facilities management). In reality these are linked, and there will be implications for how things work or how they need to change.

Being able to learn about and iterate services based on outside-in performance is, in the words of Matt Edgar (service transformation director in NHS England), 'the last target operating model you'll ever need'.[7]

Iterate towards the capabilities and people needed

Lara Sampson[8] refers to a more dynamic operating model, meaning decisions that are based on iteration and learning and that realistically need to evolve over time. As Lara says, 'it's not a jigsaw to be fitted together'.

It's possible to iterate towards a better operating model – it's just not a good idea to start by defining the end. That said, some capabilities take time to establish: a new office, a change in staffing, or procuring physical infrastructure. So people want the answers sooner. But this assumes it's better to know an answer than to figure out the right or good-enough answer, and this says something about the culture. There's almost always a safer way to learn, iterate and become more certain beforehand, rather than predicting it all at the outset. Learning what's needed to operate and by when goes hand in hand with choosing the right delivery approach (discussed in chapter 6).

This approach requires a commitment to basing choices on evidence, not conjecture. The questions that need to be answered will emerge in more detail as teams do the work. The following steps form a basic model.

- Identify the questions you need to answer along the way, and by when you might need some initial estimates or answers to start with. For example: What capabilities will we need? Where will people operate from? Who will we need? How might this change over time or with scale? What's the most important or urgent thing to know?
- Plan very simply the work needed to answer these questions. What to do to more accurately learn and then do what's needed, to know what the better or right answers are, and to provide constructive challenge and implications for any assumed or predetermined answers.
- Set up people and teams to be able to learn and make the right decisions or recommendations.

- Learn by putting in place some of the parts that are needed quickly, to learn and to move on from. Work with very small numbers of people, users or cases to do this safely, and iterate from there. Protect the ability to have a way out or to reverse a decision if it's not working well.

Manage improvements to existing services

Much of this book has focused on how to influence 'change' that is already happening – all the pieces of work, projects, programmes, portfolios –in such a way as to have the best possible impact on services and outcomes (or to prevent that change negatively affecting them).

Important services need to be directly developed and improved on an ongoing basis, rather than waiting for opportunities for one-off improvements. Live services generate their own work. There are many issues and sudden priorities that will come up when running services, in addition to ongoing performance improvement. Balancing the priorities requires ongoing leadership, coordination and funding across the whole, not just for the existing operations part (sometimes referred to as 'business-as-usual', or 'BAU', in traditional organizations) – or just the part that is undergoing change.

For this you need the right processes and people in place to manage and prioritize the work most likely to contribute significant value.

Establish organizing principles and parameters

Find a way of codifying the most important thing to achieve that those who are prioritizing can keep front of mind. For example: 'Prioritize what will deliver the job of the service and the desired outcome most efficiently.' For a prisoner probation programme, the outcome could be to reduce reoffending, which might mean teams focusing on learning what is most likely to impact reoffending rates[9] instead of just carrying on doing the same things they've always done. For mature services the priority is often to improve efficiency.

Prioritize service changes together

Make sure the people prioritizing changes to services over the short term and the long term (e.g. the next 2–4 weeks or the next 12–24 months) represent all relevant disciplines, particularly those closest to the services affected, to users and to operations. You can follow up with other relevant governance processes once you have a strong steer from those with the context, who are basing their direction on evidence.

Give teams the ability to say no

Operating teams should be able to say no, or strongly recommend against doing something if it might cause significant problems or if there's a lack of capacity. It helps build trust and safety. One way to do this is to make proposals visible to all and give certain people or teams the ability to vote or comment. Create a process that takes this feedback and makes sure it is actioned or discussed.

Intentionally design the comms and training processes

For many services, the overall design or the design of different parts will evolve over time. There's often work underway to make a service easier to operate or to make parts of it more efficient for internal staff. This means changes for operations. As part of the conditions for ongoing service improvement, we need to consider the 'learning journey' of everyone involved in the service from start to finish. This also means anticipating and responding to learning needs. This could include

- embedding the expectation that internal staff will regularly look at new guidance to see what's changed in the service;
- making sure that communications actually work for people providing the service, e.g. whether people are able to absorb daily updates to operations and working out what the right frequency for updates is;
- understanding what operational staff need to be able to support customers with complex needs;
- designing tools so that operations can do what's needed, or so they know the right details to be able to help customers; and
- figuring out how to support self-service in terms of learning, rather than pushing out every detail for every role or activity affected to everyone's individual inboxes.

Develop services with the people who operate them

It's easy to create problems and inefficiencies for people who operate services if we're not aware of all the implications when service decisions or priorities are set.

In many cases, staff have previously been left with awful tools to manage significant volumes of work. It can take quite a while to build trust and to see how different it can be when everyone about all aspects of services, including what it's like for staff to operate, and works together to improve it all.

Establish ways for staff to share feedback so that it is actioned. This could include problems, ideas and suggestions across the overall service, or it could be just the tools used by internal staff. Set up a process to triage the suggestions or requests and theme it into actionable chunks for delivery teams or leadership. Staff can tell service teams about things that aren't working and help identify improvements. They could use tools to raise tickets with teams who can make changes. People need to be available to work with the teams receiving that feedback and insight, to help group or theme suggestions and issues, to find the right channel for them, and to work together to address them. Help people see the direct benefits of ownership and involvement by communicating what happened as a result of their vote, feedback, contribution or suggestion. Make 'getting input from operational teams first' one of the criteria to prioritize work across the service.

Some services establish 'ambassadors': people working with one foot in service change and delivery and the other in day-to-day operations. These ambassadors work with service teams and have the power to argue the case for prioritizing changes for internal staff, or to say no to a particular design direction if it will result in greater effort than there is capacity for.

Champion the support needed for healthy operations

Practices like these need championing. For some organizations this is a significant change to normal operations. It rests on having good leaders and directors who recognize that old ways of working hamper the ability to change, and then actually take the action needed to operate differently.

Some organizations establish teams to support the transformation of operational working practice, to help secure the conditions needed for continuous improvement. These teams instigate procedures such as protecting time each week for people to catch up on learning, or for leaders to have conversations with staff to embed changes. They release operational people to work as part of service change teams. This gives staff opportunities for operational career development that wouldn't necessarily happen otherwise. Because this relies on having up-to-date operational knowledge, it puts career opportunities in reach of people at any level, not just those of a certain seniority. It provides the potential for progression by giving experience of new ways of working that are becoming the norm in modern service organizations.

Summary

① Make a simple, wrong plan. Frequently improve it and add more details as you know more.

② Identify what needs to be learned across a service, and how that is expected to happen.

③ Explore the potential showstoppers as early on as possible, not down the line in a sequential plan.

④ An operating model means who and what you need, doing what and where. Iterate your way towards this, by starting small, basing decisions on real evidence, and being prepared to evolve the model over time

⑤ Establish processes that involve those who operate the service with the work to change or deliver parts of it differently. This means prioritizing together, having votes for or against, and creating feedback loops with operations.

Iterating the design and operating model while delivering the service

NHS COVID-19 vaccination service, England

In March 2020 vaccines – and services for people to get vaccinated – were needed as quickly as possible. James Spirit is head of product and Tero Väänänen is head of design at NHS England. James shares what happened between April and December 2020 during the coronavirus pandemic to create England's NHS COVID-19 vaccination service:[10]

> We quickly got into the end-to-end journey. It wasn't going to be just about booking an appointment, it was how do we make people aware, and it was the whole operational side: how we get

supplies in, how do we know when supplies are there and where they are, how to make sure the experience was safe. We had to manage demand too; there were specific cohorts of people set by the UK government via the Joint Committee on Vaccination and Immunisation, and the service had to be consistent with that. This included how we identify people, how we check eligibility, how we check their vaccination history and how we match them with the right vaccination type. The 'requirements' became very complicated.

Different NHS organizations led the operational deployment, the coordination, and the 'delivery' of enabling technology and data. In the early days of the programme, it was assumed all the requirements would be gathered up-front and then handed over to different teams to deliver the service. But the requirements were too long, too complicated; we wouldn't have been able to deliver a working service in time – or to adapt to what might be ahead of us.

We had a single imperative to get people to vaccination appointments by December 2020. We had to change the approach and put everyone's focus on the outcome – maximize the number of people getting a vaccine as soon as possible, by creating the simplest possible version of the service and removing all potential barriers.

The team had direct access to operational people who were running the vaccination programme, strategy people, policy people, clinical people, comms people, as well as other staff in the vaccination sites, general practices and pharmacies.

Tero explains:

Whilst designing the service, we were very aware of the health professionals and other staff who were running the service in large vaccination sites, General Practices and pharmacies, and we made sure to also research their needs and challenges. For example, what systems did they use and how, what paper-based processes were in use and how could we make some of those more digital. Clinical safety is paramount when designing for health and care; a simple usability issue on a system could cause wrong data to be entered by accident, recorded into the person's medical record and thus create clinical risk. Usability truly is a clinical safety issue.

The team delivered a complex, critical national service within eight months; this required creating the conditions for teams to focus on the imperative, while tackling all barriers in the way, which included some of the traditional decision making structures.

James describes some of the changes to governance processes:

We removed the layers of hierarchy, the paperwork, the meetings. Instead, it was 'the teams will come to you with specific questions and decisions we need to make so we can keep on track – and if we don't get a decision, we agree that we'll make one between us'. Having that rapid decision making process is what made this possible. There were different levels of multidisciplinary decision makers meeting multiple times a day, so that nothing would be held up.

The end-to-end service was mapped out from start to finish, rather than focusing solely on the technology. Data points within the supply chain fed right back into booking appointments and sending appointments to people. For instance, before sending 1 million letters out the next day, we'd check the capacity in the booking system; it was dynamic that way, which meant a trade-off between the imperative to get bookings done now, with the time to get the messaging and perception right, which was a challenge.

At busy times we've supported over a million people booking an appointment on a single day. We've achieved real scale. And we see opportunities to expand it to other kinds of appointments.

> Under normal circumstances, teams could be told what to do upfront, with four-year business plans and tons of paperwork and board meetings going back and forth nailing down scope, and then when it hits reality you realize you need to change everything, and you have to go through funding processes again.
>
> It couldn't have worked this way for the vaccination service. The pandemic has resulted in a permanent change to our ways of working across organizations and across disciplines.

Continuous development and improvement of a live service
DWP, Universal Credit, UK

Universal Credit is a live service and millions of people use it. It continues to be developed. New code is released every week, which means managing an ongoing cycle of change rather than working to a one-off plan. It requires ongoing communications, learning and feedback from internal users and frontline staff, in addition to testing what works and doesn't work with customers. To manage continuous change at this scale, they needed a process for gathering feedback, and ways to support regularly rolling out changes to the service across such a large operation. Deb Boore, transformation and delivery director, Universal Credit, DWP, explains how they created a network of people they called service innovation leads (SILs) to help, placing them in each Jobcentre and telephony service centre.[11]

> They are digital and service experts who were able to coach other staff in using the service. They were put on site to help with training and with questions from colleagues. But they quickly became an important part of the whole product support lifecycle. Our front-line staff raise both incidents and suggestions through this network. The SILs triage these based on their own knowledge to determine whether it's a known or new issue, a valid suggestion, or a learning need. They feed up this intelligence as part of

product support, to be fixed, impacted, or to go onto our back-log for future releases. And then they go back to the person who raised it, with updates. It means that staff feel they have a voice in how the service develops.

Coordinating this level of change at scale requires collective and active leadership. Each new release could mean fixes, changes to the process or to the service itself, or to what customers see and use. Deb describes their current working practice as a cycle:

On a Friday we finalize what's going into production. On a Monday we send a leaders note and a 'feature update notice' which are summaries of the changes, setting out what they mean for differ-ent job roles, with links to instructions and guidance about what we need people to do differently. We also have Tuesday calls with the SILs and operational leaders, where we go into more detail, so they can support colleagues on the ground. Time is set aside in offices for communicating the changes, and we always go to a handful of sites to ask people if they've seen or heard the comms and whether they can find it on the internal hub where all our comms and guidance are. We make it everyone's responsibility to keep themselves up to date, whether that's individually or as a group. Recently, we've created a new communications and assur-ance role at site level. They will check that people know where to find the information they need, and that they're really looking at stuff – and if they're not, someone is telling them or helping them to. It's about getting to everybody, to make sure that we get the best from the service and can give the right information to customers.

Chapter 9

Establish whole-service leadership

The biggest change is often encouraging leaders to care about what other leaders care about.

When dozens of teams are at work on services, success relies on cohesion. Ideally this comes from the right team types, working together more permanently, using modern working practice that's underpinned by clarity and unity – all while knowing what other teams are doing and how it all relates. But until this is working well and sustainably in your organization, it requires hands-on coordination and leadership across the whole. Typically, though, leadership is structured within individual functions rather than across services.

Leadership of individual professions (e.g. product, operations, policy, user-centred design) can find that most of their time and attention goes on growing and managing that profession, rather than on directing and influencing services and strategy.

It's no longer enough to just hope it's all managed sensibly. Given how important services are and how much they are changing, this chapter shows how to pair important leadership characteristics from across different functions and professions, to create leadership of the whole.

Whole-service leadership

Whole-service leadership entails a culture of people feeling and behaving like one cohesive team, working together in pursuit of the same goals, and providing constructive challenge from the reality of their experience. What makes a leadership team, as opposed to a group of separate individuals, is the ability to work together. Leading together for the good of the whole isn't a natural state in larger older organizations. Because existing leadership tends to mirror the separation of functions and cost centres, there's no one obvious place to find the individuals that are best suited, or have the most relevant experience, to lead a whole service. It depends on leaders having particular attitudes, beliefs and behaviours, in addition to translatable skills and experience.

Whole-service leadership can be an uncomfortable fit for other reasons too. Unless the overall structure changes, these new individuals or roles will overlap with existing leadership. Some overlap is powerful and strengthens the teams with collaborative mindsets, but it also changes power structures.

The introduction of the role of chief digital officer (CDO) alongside an existing chief information officer (CIO) or chief technology officer (CTO) has been contentious in some places. Organizations haven't always handled the process well, with individuals left to fight it out until someone 'wins', or to carve out individual responsibility between them. This means people end up leading individual parts rather than leading together across the whole.

Service organizations need leaders

- who have organization and/or industry domain knowledge;
- who are aware enough and recognize the importance of modern approaches to technology, data and human-centred design; and
- whose attitude and behaviour demonstrates that they actively care about the whole and that they work collaboratively.

You can usually find leaders with two of these three characteristics. Pairing people to cover the three together can be the best approach in the short term.

Whole-service leadership activities
Anyone involved in attempts to transform a service in a way that doesn't include operational leadership will know the flaws of this approach. 'Business as usual' gets its name because it's viewed by some as not being involved in 'design and change'. But this unhelpfully separates those that know most about the reality of running the service from those with the power to change how it runs.

This section provides leadership activities and structures to help organizations choreograph work across the whole, taking into account all angles. Lara Sampson talks about four important aspects for service leadership, which I've built on here.

1. *Holding the overall vision for the entire service* on behalf of users, potential users, operations and internal users. Including in this vision the policy intent and organization outcomes, as well as what's needed in terms of technology or data. Using this to drive the right work, to prioritize, to protect or challenge, to push back and to negotiate.

2. *Knowing how to lead change operationally.* This means understanding the domain and the details well enough to build trust from operational and compliance people, but at the same time being able to see in abstract how it could work very differently. Critically, knowing how to get things done within your organization in support of the overall vision – which makes it likely that they'll have been there for a while.

3. *Communicating outwards and upwards,* so that everyone is clear about what's happening, what the priorities are, how it's working, and why decisions are being made. This means

understanding but also challenging and negotiating with senior leadership, executives, board members, politicians, regulators or lobbying parties. Acting to protect the vision, the deliverability or the ways of working. An important part of this is reinforcing the need for change (to services and/ or ways of working), and providing constructive backup to others.

4. *Corralling the various people who influence strategy or policy or who 'own' outcomes* to be able to clarify direction and impact for everyone working towards it. The right leadership helps protect and defend the vision, the teams, the work in hand and the deliverability while skilfully supporting the development of new ideas at the right time and managing changes in priority to achieve them.

These four sets of activities go hand in hand. Across a very large and complex service this could be four individuals working incredibly closely together. Acting as one to escalate shared challenges to the right people is more powerful than doing it alone. In other situations it could be one leader with collective responsibility across functions.

Leadership titles vary. You could translate these activities into existing roles, or you could use them to set out desired capabilities or entirely new service leadership roles.

Although these activities can't be done well by just anyone. There can't be a bias towards either digital and technology change, design or operational change. They aren't easily standardized into a professional framework. If the wrong person is in post, they won't give the right steer to everyone else, or collaborate well, and that will have an enormous impact on the service or programme success. Whole-service leadership means taking and making the space for all that's required to bring about the desired change, understanding the close connection between what works well for people on the outside – the users – and how well arranged the parts are on the inside. Service leaders need to be open to finding out what works.

If you're in the position of starting a new major service from scratch, you can establish service leadership from the start. If there's an existing context, identify the best-suited individuals to lead among equals.

Service leadership is not the same as 'customer journey' or 'customer experience' leadership
The idea of organizing leadership horizontally around customer journeys has existed for many years.[1] But this often results in leadership only for the parts of services that are exposed to customers – the websites, apps, outgoing communications or customer accounts – and not for the supporting capabilities, technology and processes underneath, all of which are fundamental to how well a service works inside and out.

Whole-service leadership includes all the parts that contribute to the success of that service. This includes the bits that are user-facing as well as day-to-day operations and the technology and processes that support them – and the strategy or policy that gives them direction. Note that none of the leadership activities above mentions 'owning' these things. The role is that of being a lead, a guardian or someone who holds the vision for it all, on behalf of the service, with support from specialists.

Coordinating work across whole services

When much is changing, it can require day-to-day coordination in addition to leadership across the whole.

This means people with the time to spend with teams, as well as in meetings, observing what's going on, being more consistently available, and being able to detect and translate significant issues for leadership. These are the people who can provide a steer with the bigger picture in mind, while being able to flesh out more detailed issues so that others can help form immediate plans of action.

Typical coordinating activities include

- creating, maintaining and communicating a view of services and performance – how they're changing over time, the work that is needed, the teams involved or the changes planned;
- spending time with teams to know when to intervene or steer work in progress, to shape new work, to adjust structure, or to understand and help with issues or changes in direction;
- creating roadmaps and plans to help others to understand what's happening now and what's happening later, and why, and to help protect the time and space for teams to do what's needed; and
- anticipating the problems and doing the legwork to develop solutions or to help escalate when there's a need for tough decisions or for the protection of teams by leadership (sometimes called 'managing upwards').

Service-coordinating teams often include professional leads from different disciplines. Some specialisms need to be well represented here because of the nature of the work or because of a blind spot in the organization.

Two very useful people to be involved are:

- Someone who understands technology and can 'translate' for others, such as by anticipating, identifying, exploring and laying out the significant issues around technology, data, security, interoperability and other standards, future trends and the need for resilience, in non-technical terms. This can be done by a good technical lead from within an existing service team. But when there are multiple teams changing different parts of a technologically complex service, a trusted technical lead with time to spend with other teams and be available to advise leadership is extremely valuable – so long as they remain grounded in the reality of what will work best for users and operations.

- Someone who understands the whole service – and particularly the lifelong journey and the reality of experience for users – who spends time observing research with real users and has the experience and contextual awareness to anticipate what is likely to cause problems. They have the necessary skills to help everyone involved identify and then agree to tackle the gaps in plans. This involves being able to hold the bigger vision in mind, but with an eye for detail to point out the one ambiguous sentence that will result in lots of calls to the contact centre. This is often a user researcher, content designer, product manager or service designer.

These leadership and coordinating roles and activities can also be extremely valuable across programmes or portfolios that transcend any individual service, to help align and assure work.

Principles of good service leadership

Of course, changing leadership culture in a large organization is much more than just adding some new activities or roles. To emphasize the different behaviours and ways of working that are needed, and to highlight what's expected, it can be a good idea to establish some leadership principles. This can make the differences more tangible for those who are used to working highly independently.

Here are some pointers to consider.

- Whole-service leadership involves the guardianship of issues and opportunities on behalf of the whole, sharing responsibility for what's important. It's not about establishing or maintaining individual power or control. For this to be practical, it could mean appointing leads for each important theme who work on behalf of a group of equals, not a single owner who can exclude others.

- Doing the job well means constructively challenging each other, the constraints and any unhelpful practice, involving people with the means and experience to recognize the problems. If you find that leadership agrees or defers on everything, rather than robustly discussing and challenging each other for the good of the whole, that indicates a problem.

- Be 'in service' to the teams that are delivering (to an extent), because 'doing' is where most of the value is. Do everything possible to protect, defend and unblock teams. And be prepared to make fast 'good enough' decisions to avoid holding up progress – and be able to intuit when it's worth waiting for the (more) right answer.

- Be able and prepared to tackle the uncomfortable, difficult problems that don't have obvious trade-offs; make the hard choices to protect and defend whatever is the most important thing to get done.

- Be directional when necessary. Even teams set up to be relatively autonomous will need clear direction from leadership from time to time. For example:
  - to know what they can communicate outwards on sensitive topics,
  - to make a decision about a tricky or non-obvious issue, or
  - to get an action or direction unblocked.

You'll want to define your own version with others, so that there is a sense of ownership. Use the above as a starting point for discussion. It won't guarantee that everyone will buy into this, but it does form something more objective to point to if it's not working in these ways. Share it with senior leaders to set their expectations.

Service leadership as a profession

The UK government recognizes a professional role of 'service owner'.[2] This has helped establish the need for people to look across all the teams delivering work. There are now some brilliant individual service owners who work on genuine end-to-end services across the UK government as a result.

Adapt for the reality of how the service operates
Many large services have complex commercial arrangements to navigate. They require people with the skills and experience to manage suppliers, in addition to caring about performance across the whole. Some of these commercial arrangements will hamper a service's ability to iterate and respond quickly. The model infers distance between those who commission work and those who do the work. But it's also the reality for some organizations and some large services today. It might be the best choice, or it might simply be unavoidable in some situations.

Yet some of these organizations are also taking steps towards whole-service ownership, starting from where they're at. They set out the reality of what is needed but pave the way for genuine horizontal leadership across the whole. For a service that has a complex or partly outsourced delivery model, leadership might be responsible for

- developing and maintaining a performant and compliant service; monitoring and managing risk; directing work across the service;
- acting as the point of contact for the direction the service is moving in; representing the organization; providing a view to suppliers of the service about what good looks like; coordinating and supporting investment; and

- identifying and driving change; commissioning work; directing work as the main sponsor; managing suppliers and partners in terms of service performance and evolution.

The experience of using some large services will vary significantly depending on the situation people are in. Some organizations split service leadership to focus on groups of people who might share needs, behaviours or prior experiences, to strengthen what works for them – or to avoid what doesn't.

Be bold about what good service leadership looks like
All that said, be confident about what is really needed. Don't stop yourself from stating what good looks like for service leadership, even if the organization you work with is very far away from adopting this as a model. You can hold this view while still acknowledging that there is always a starting point from which to evolve and improve over time.

Antipatterns to watch out for

Leadership structures that support whole services can still honour the responsibilities and accountabilities set out by the organization or for a sector. But it's also true that individuals can use the appearance of overlap and conflict to protect the status quo.

A few common examples below help expose the difference.

Hierarchy, competition and separation
Organizations often talk about the need to trust, collaborate with and respect one another and to avoid hierarchy but without taking any decisive actions that make these things happen. Individuals continue to work separately or don't fully trust each other. They represent their own function, interest or practice rather than what's needed across the whole. There's often a lack of healthy interaction and constructive challenge. People aren't

listened to or involved unless they're of a certain seniority, or within a certain group, which puts distance between those who contribute to decisions and those who have recent experience of the reality of day-to-day operations and of users.

An impossible task
Sometimes a person is asked to own a service that's too large and complex for any one individual to hold in their head in sufficient detail. Simultaneously, they're expected to lead the vision, change operations, support business as usual, unblock delivery teams, negotiate and navigate the rest of the organization and the investment cases, change ways of working and communicate outwards and upwards. They're set up to only do some parts well, or to fail altogether – or even to burn out.

A project not a service
People are asked to be a service owner for what is really a one-off project or an individual team working continuously on a feature, tool or system. It isn't a whole service. In reality, their role is closer to a project manager, product manager or workstream lead. This might be appropriate for the context, it might be a good place to start, and there might be excellent people in the role, but it's not the same as end-to-end whole-service leadership.

Change that's separate to operation
This is where someone is asked to own the one-off modernization of a service but not the service as a whole. This could involve overseeing temporary delivery teams or suppliers, with the expectation of handing over to operations to run the service or to IT to maintain the technology. This is more akin to a traditional temporary workstream or programme lead, or a technology-focused product manager. They might bring good practice to the development of these component parts of a service, but for this to work, they'll need to find ways to remove the hand-off culture, integrate operations, fund continuous

improvement and encourage everyone to care about the performance of the whole service, end to end.

Keeping the day job
Another common scenario is where the existing leadership, the senior person responsible or a sponsor is asked to be a 'service owner' or leader, on top of their other responsibilities – often with no additional training and guidance, without any expectations being set, and without changes to the way existing processes and governance work. They won't have the time to hold the detail and direct the work in any way that's different to a traditional hands-off leadership role. This is not service leadership. Expectations need to be set about what this role entails. If it's to be filled by someone with existing duties, their current activities need to be scaled back to allow them to get much closer to what's happening.

*

Work with others to establish and protect the right leadership for services. I recommend setting out the leadership activities and the differences, to make clear what's needed and to win support for it. Don't just add a new person or role to the mix and expect them to change the whole organization single-handedly.

Encourage people to work together across services

You don't have to wait for the right leadership to be in place before taking steps to create more supportive conditions. There are other ways to support people working together for better services. Community leadership can start with finding other people who are involved and developing a shared understanding of where a service could go, who is doing what, and where the opportunities are to collaborate to improve it. There are many helpful guides on how to establish and maintain communities, including Emily Webber's *Building Successful Communities of Practice.*[3]

Two of the ways in which individuals within organizations have brought service communities together are

1. establishing informal networks of people who work across the same service but who come from different teams, functions or even organizations; and

2. bringing together communities of people who work on the same part or same capability of different services to share ideas, e.g. everyone working on digital identity, caseworking or application forms.

1. Networks of people working across one service

The UK government created groups it called 'service communities'.[4] These are networks of people around a shared service, a shared outcome, a common 'pathway' or 'user journey', or a shared interest in helping users in a specific situation. This could help to create a more joined-up approach across the boundaries of organizations and functions ahead of any formal agreements or roles if it involves the right people – people who have leverage – meeting often enough. Once you find a few interested individuals, you can start by building a map of the whole service together so that everyone starts to understand who does what. Sketch a view of all the activity and change across the service. Informal networks like these can help connect teams, align work with what good looks like overall, and tackle some of the important problems or gaps across the whole.

2. People working on one part of many services

Some services follow a similar pattern, which makes it valuable to share work and ideas about specific capabilities or parts of a service. In one example, a regular gathering brought together everyone involved in designing and improving 'casework systems' in or between organizations.[5] In another organization, it's people who work on ways to prove and verify identity digitally. Useful activities include showing work in progress, sharing problems and opportunities, or getting wider support on how to tackle issues.

Summary

① Whole-service leadership is a fundamental change from leading separate functions and parts to operating as a genuine team to connect and coordinate work across services.

② Leaders need to be able to hold the vision, lead operational change, communicate upwards and outwards, and corral influencing parties to protect the priorities.

③ Agree principles to set expectations for service leadership and activities. Identify leadership antipatterns to help your organization understand and set conditions for success.

④ You don't need to wait for the right leadership. Establish informal networks of people across services to work together to build shared views and collaborate to improve how it works. This could be a one-off workshop or a regular meet-up.

Service managers across an end-to-end service
HM Passport Office, UK
HM Passport Office is the issuer of UK passports and is responsible for civil registration services in England and Wales through the General Register Office.

Colin Foley, head of business and service design, describes how the role of end-to-end service manager has developed and evolved, and how improvement work across the service is currently prioritized by a 'quartet' of disciplines.[6] The quartet includes an operational service manager, a digital service owner, a business architect or a service designer, and a technical architect.

As we began to manage the end-to-end service delivered to the customer we developed a role we called 'operational service manager'. We already had digital service owners, but they were actually focused on digital products such as online applications or digital caseworking, alongside supplier managers and marketing efforts.

The operational service managers understand how the service is performing on a day-to-day basis, holding customer needs in mind, and working with all the other parts of the business to say 'this needs to knit together', 'we have a performance issue here', or to prioritize a particular problem or issue. It means you have someone always looking at the whole service, with oversight of supplier relationships, day-to-day contract management and performance management, who works with casework teams and customer services who support all of our services. They hold the overall view and work closely with the digital service owners and the business design authority for larger changes or improvements we need to make strategically. They also coordinate the overall response if there's a continuity issue. Another part of it is working closely with information providers to gather insight, whether that's customer insight, public protection, business intelligence or user research.

They make sure the whole service joins up for the purpose of delivering to the customer; being that voice across the whole piece, so that everyone knows what we're meant to be achieving. The service managers are coordinating it all, across different customer segments or variations of the main service. They're supported by enabling functions and capabilities that form the foundations of the service, and a service delivery director that leads it overall.

Characteristics of a good service leader

Eileen Logie is an experienced service leader. She describes some of the characteristics that have helped her to lead complex and high-profile services.[7]

You can't be distant. You need to be a hands-on delivery person, as far as you can be with a few hundred staff and dozens of teams. It's about working together, with common goals and milestones. You need to understand what you're trying to achieve overall, and then create a structure where teams are working as efficiently as possible towards this. You're often making significant cultural changes across the organization too, sometimes with people who aren't used to working on services end to end in this way. You need to lead from the front, helping everyone constantly think about where we are going, reflecting on the why, and on the value, for our customers and for us. It means being at the whiteboard with people, working together to reprioritize delivery, especially in the face of massive and urgent changes; for example, figuring out how we give eligible people money within the next twelve weeks. Situations like the pandemic force you to find ways to bypass all the historic problems.

I could be leading twelve or fifteen digital teams at any one time, who are working on different transactional parts of a service, while other teams are looking at support models or helping to coordinate user research and content design. There are often other specialists too, for example optimizing how people find the service and get set up to use it. Service leadership is a combination of vision and prioritization, as well as developing the right daily routines. It means managing budgets to be able to support ongoing delivery and improvement, as well as the right procurement routes to be able to support the kind of service growth I'm often leading. All while learning what's needed to optimally shift from creating a service from scratch, to scaling and improving a live service.

Equal leadership and making decisions together

DWP, Universal Credit, UK

Deb Boore, transformation and delivery director, Universal Credit, DWP, describes the value of leadership being hands-on, to be able to govern and make prioritization decisions efficiently.[8]

There needs to be equal voices in design and prioritization, and a balance of focus on the experience of customers and colleagues alongside policy, security and service stability. In the beginning, we had a genuinely multidisciplinary team, based in a single location, who cared about the whole service. We came from different disciplines but weren't just subject matter experts – you came into this team, you brought with you your skillset and the knowledge that you have but you weren't constrained by your job title or grade. You were an empowered decision maker for the part of the world you came from – whether that was policy, operations or finance – but once in the room you brought your whole self to the team. We all made decisions on behalf of the whole, as well as on behalf of our part of the business. Of course, we had all the right conversations with our networks too, but we were in that room to make decisions.

That model has of course evolved as the service grew in complexity, but those principles remain. They were the conditions we created to be able to rapidly learn and develop based on evidence, and we still hold true to that way of working, despite working across multiple locations now, and even, through the Covid pandemic, from our homes.

Bringing service providers together to solve known problems

Citizens Advice, UK

Citizens Advice provides confidential information and advice to assist people with legal, debt, consumer, benefits, housing and other problems in the UK. They also gather evidence about the problems people face with services across the UK.

Citizens Advice had evidence that some letters that energy suppliers send to customers about debt and complaints weren't working. Customers didn't fully understand the letters, they felt intimidated, and they didn't know what to do next. This meant the energy companies weren't getting the money they were owed, while their complaints processes had backlogs.

Working with the energy regulator OFGEM, Citizens Advice gathered representatives from across the main energy companies for a working session on making service improvements, including specialists from compliance and regulatory teams.

They shared research about the problems customers faced with energy services.[9] Together they created a set of principles for how letters can be worded more simply and clearly, including how to test content with users to check if it's understandable. They then prototyped different kinds of letters applying these new principles, working as teams. This provided stimulus for energy providers to test with their own customers and to improve how this part of their service works.

Chapter 10

Steer programmes and portfolios to deliver outcomes

Making better services involves setting teams outcomes that are free of implied solutions.[1] But we still need to know if the work is on the right path or not, if it's valuable, who needs more support, or where to intervene.

One recent study of large IT programmes showed that fewer than 20% of them were deemed successful.[2] With those odds it could seem as though success is a happy accident. But you don't have to hope for large programmes to be successful. You can design for it.

When organizations struggle to see a service as a whole, they don't see the problem with splitting up work into one-off changes, treating it as if it is all entirely separate. On the one hand, you need 'team-shaped' problems to have a hope of actually delivering something. But on the other, separation can discourage the 'working together' that is often needed to achieve desired outcomes as a whole.

A programme is a collection of related projects and teams. Traditional programme management proposes that projects are defined upfront and aligned in a specific sequence, and that managers ensure that outputs are delivered within budget and on time.[3] On face value, this doesn't allow for testing and learning what will result in the desired outcomes, or for changing course to achieve them. But if the outputs or timelines can't always be fixed down, how can you know if you're doing the right work – or whether it's on track?

It's natural for people to worry about large programmes. What's valuable is offering practical support and expertise to address the problems.

This chapter shares practical ideas to bring clarity to what are often many confusing pieces of work. It's a series of techniques to gear up programmes and portfolios to deliver outcomes, not just one-off changes.

Do what's important faster, by doing less

Some organizations will add more work as the default answer to problems rather than reducing the amount of work to give priorities proper attention. As Chris Fleming (a partner at Public Digital) put it:[4] 'Strategy is making hard choices, explaining trade-offs, delivering on priorities. Strategy is not looking at

Figure 9. A deep dive on new ideas or work in progress.

all ... you are doing and identifying some themes that vaguely stitch them together.'

It can be difficult to persuade people that one of the problems is simply too much going on in the first place, especially if they're not close enough to the work or don't care enough about it to acknowledge the risks.

A valuable activity for leaders and other specialists is to spend a few days digging into the details of all the work in progress, together. This immersion helps to gain an impression about what is strong and what is unclear, to learn from each other's perspectives, and to be aware of what most closely matches priorities.

What you cover together could include the following.

- What the work is, as well as its component parts. Ask teams to put it clearly and simply, as if describing the work to someone who doesn't know what the organization does.
- Whether there are any pressing deadlines, commitments or priorities.
- What the potential impact is. You can rate this from higher to lower across a set of dimensions, e.g. the value for users, the relative importance of outcomes, deliverability, and whether it results in more modern capabilities that make adapting to change easier in future.
- Compare the overall value or impact with the certainty we have. Have we made the effort to learn all we can, have we evidence that backs it up, or is there still more to learn? Doing this across a number of pieces of work helps clarify where teams are strong and where help is needed.
- Decide the boldest possible recommendation that, as a group, you can bear to make about this work. If you needed to decide today, would you wind it down, merge it with something else, do it a bit later instead, change the effort in some other way, ask for some further analysis, encourage focus on what isn't certain, or continue with it as it is?

Develop a clear relationship between outcomes and work in progress

To develop a view of a programme's or a portfolio's chance of success, you need a way to connect the work being delivered to the high-level direction or strategy. This won't make all the work magically align, but it will form a stronger basis to assess whether it's on the right path or not. This assessment doesn't need to be complicated. It can start with something as simple as asking the team involved why they think they're doing this work. Or it can be formalized by introducing a regular process to score work against objective criteria.

The example I share here has the added benefit of providing leadership with a single-page view of the entire programme, which makes it easier for them to explain what's going on to others – or to challenge it.

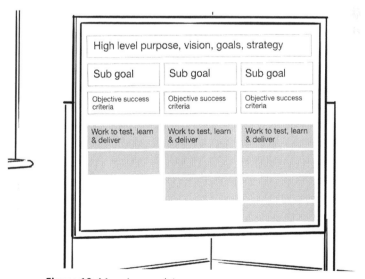

Figure 10. Mapping work in progress to assess outcomes.

High-level direction: goals, vision or strategy
Aim for a few sentences that describe what the organization, pro-gramme or portfolio is trying to achieve. This might be a written vision, a set of outcomes or a strategy. You'll find examples of these in business cases and other documents. Inevitably, you'll be working with a mixed bag of statements at different levels: strat-egy, goals, aims, objectives, plans and so on. Don't worry if it's not very clear at this point, so long as people find it recognizable. The next layer down provides a chance for making it more specific.
Here are some examples.

- *Outcomes or goals.* 'Achieve net zero carbon emissions.' 'Increase productivity for an industry.' 'Get more small businesses to pay the right tax.' 'Increase equity of wealth distribution.'
- *Strategy.* 'Create the platforms to be able to provide different kinds of financial support to an industry for the next decade.' 'Do everything possible so that our clients don't have to do anything at all.'
- *High-level metrics or targets.* 'Thirty percent of potential users participating within three years.' 'Reduce the time it takes to reach an agreement from three months to one week.'

Subgoals
Break the high-level direction into more manageable chunks. For example:

- increase the number of people participating;
- free up advisor time to support customers with more com-plex situations;
- make it operationally sustainable and reduce cost to serve;
- make services that users want to use and that make it possi-ble to do what's needed to achieve goals;
- encourage participants to contribute and to be involved in the community;

- create the culture, modern capabilities and processes to be able to adapt and improve services in future;
- encourage users to migrate from an old service to a new one;
- reallocate land resources towards optimal environmental uses.

This level of detail is more instructive about the kind of work that's most likely to contribute.

Objective success criteria
Success criteria tell us something about how we'd know if we were on the right path. They help us be more intuitive about whether proposed work is more or less likely to contribute to goals. In many cases it's preferable and safer to make and prove gradual progress than it is to wait until the end to see if it was worth it.

These success criteria don't have to be indicators or metrics; they could be objective (or objective-ish) statements.

For example, one might have 'Create the foundations and processes to be able to adapt to changing priorities' as the goal. The success criteria could then include

- the presence of permanent teams able to learn and iterate,
- the introduction of modern technology and processes, and
- teams adopting new ways of working.

Or the goal could be 'Make the service operationally sustainable'. The success criteria might then include

- a reduced cost per transaction or per change or improvement to aim for over time,
- the number of iterations and improvements to operational tools,
- a reduction in the time needed for common tasks or situations, and
- indicators of improvements to a compliance regime.

How to learn and/or deliver

This part describes the actual work that is being done – something that's often missing in other frameworks or views. It would be easy to fall into the trap of listing all the names of the teams or projects and technology being developed, which are hard to relate back to goals and high-level direction. (Although if they are hard to relate, that's already revealing.) Instead, try describing the work according to what it is (or should be) trying to learn or achieve. Some examples:

- Develop a way to make regular payments to organizations that work towards improving productivity.
- Learn how to encourage users to invest in productivity equipment and processes.
- Create a way to show users what's available to them or what they need to do to apply for something.
- Develop a way for analysts to explore data and make connections that will better guide operational decision-making.
- Make it possible for people to register interest in a new product.

Such descriptions form the catalyst for teams to set out clear logic: a series of statements about why this work in particular, or the options chosen, will contribute the most towards success criteria. They also clarify what – if anything – makes us confident about this. For example:

- Has the logic been tested?
- Has it been prototyped in some way and validated with small numbers of users?
- Does it already have real users and live data that make it more compelling, or is it just a hunch or an idea?

This process will make it easier to spot where the story is weaker and needs more work, or where there is considerable risk in the logic with something that's progressing at pace.

This is intended as inspiration, not instruction. There are other ways to address the disconnect between high-level goals and work in progress. But what's described here is lightweight enough to be done quickly, while being practical enough to give direction to the teams doing the work.

Assess and track progress towards goals

Once you have the means to connect work with high-level direction, it becomes easier to assess its chances of success and its rate of progress. It's hard to challenge the direction of work, or a programme overall, without a basis on which to do it. Organizations need to know when they should

- encourage teams to keep going as they are;
- double down, or invest more in a particular part of the programme;
- take a closer look before deciding what to do; or
- intervene and make a change – or stop the work.

A good way to do this is to establish criteria that are important to your organization, and to come up with a scoring system that allows for nuanced analysis and recommendations on what areas need to improve.

Here are some starting categories to consider.

1. *Strategy and direction.* What's the potential impact on – or fit with – the overall goals, direction of travel, priorities or important standards? Is it cross cutting or in isolation? Does it make sense given the wider context or strategy? Does it depend on something else or create new problems?

2. *People, customers, users.* Is it intended to be desirable? An improvement on what is already there? Or is it about reducing negative impact? What evidence do we have about attractiveness, usefulness or take-up, or about people's

ability to handle change or to do what's needed? How much confidence do we have that this will help more people do the right thing, or that it will help people save time and effort? Where does it fit in the outside-in view of a service?

3. *Organization and operation.* What's the value to the organization, what is the cost to deliver or the cost to serve, and how does it ease operations or improve efficiency or compliance?

4. *Capability.* What's the level of change? What are the risks or benefits in terms of process, technology, data or security? Does it move us towards modern ways of working and operating? Do we have the right roles and people to make this more likely?

5. *Approach and deliverability.* How well identified and managed are the risks? Are the costs proportionate to the potential value? Is the approach or methodology that is being used appropriate for the type of work and the risk? Is enough being done to 'front-load' risk and reduce it early?

As Matti Keltanen shared with me, for each individual point, a relevant domain expert – who isn't involved directly – should analyse the work, together with the approach, and then score it. This might include a technology lead, a user-centred designer, a product manager, an architect and someone with current experience of operations. It's vital that all are seen as equals: that there's no 'dominant' profession or view of what's important. Each brings something important to bear. Doing this together can create an incredibly powerful and efficient evaluation. A small team can quickly flush out many of the visible and invisible risks and gaps in approach.

At one end of the scale is: 'All the problems are well known, with sensible plans for how to resolve them. We know exactly what will need to go on. It's all working fine.' At the other end of the scale is: 'We have no idea about this work yet. It requires further work or investigation.' Some organizations develop a red–amber–green status to reflect the level of certainty: what we are certain about; what we know something about, but not enough; and what we know next to nothing about yet.

It's important this isn't positioned as a critique of work being done by teams or to point out faults. Highlighting where there is still work to do is an incredibly useful and valuable tool. Assuming the work is valuable, the basis of assessment should be about finding ways to move from low scores to high scores, but also about improving the speed at which we help teams move from low to high over time. It should strengthen already-high-performing teams by buying them time and space for a better approach. It also helps to expose the problematic initiatives that haven't been properly challenged by people in scrutinizing roles – often because doing so requires a much deeper dive to disaggregate what's valuable work from what are personal agendas or enticing but false beliefs. Traditional coordinating and governance processes aren't designed to allow the time for those deeper dives.

This assessment is necessary wherever there are very large portfolios with high volumes of work. It's not just a score, it's a process that provides recommendations for what needs to happen and what the priorities are – a process that can ground work in terms of its impact on services.

Potential supporters of a process like this include programme leadership, board members, audit and risk committee members, and chief finance and risk officers. The UK government has a mandated 'service assessment' for each phase of its agile project life cycle, and this works in a similar way.[5]

State simply what the work is for

Writing clearer versions of the jargon project names that every organization has is an incredibly simple step – but it's one that is often missed.

Internal project names are a useful shorthand reference for a team. But to others, they obscure what the work is there to do, making it harder to understand the link with priorities or to help join things up or bring scrutiny. Chapter 4 gives guidance for reframing work to make it clear. I generally recommend pairing people: someone who understands the work together with someone who can write simply, to create clear descriptions of all the work in hand across a programme or portfolio. Content designers are particularly good at writing these descriptions. It's an easy exercise that doesn't require permission, but many others will thank you for it. Include the user or the external impact if there is one. This helps to counter the inward view that is too easy for any of us to adopt when we are working inside a team.

> **Before**: 'SDP: single data platform'
> **After**: 'Improve data – how we format, store and connect data to improve services for users. Create a new capability to introduce standards for more consistent data and support adoption across the organization.'
> **Before**: 'The Industry Productivity Fund v3'
> **After**: 'Support productivity – create a service that offers financial incentives to organizations in return for them adhering to new standards and investing in research and development to improve productivity.'

Keep the original name alongside the new one for a period of time if that helps everyone keep track.

Merge the new descriptions with those held by programme functions that already maintain lists of the work in progress. Collectively adopt a standard going forward that requires teams to describe what they do simply and clearly. It's a simple but important part of good governance practice.

Situate work in the context of services

Not every piece of work in a programme or portfolio will be part of a service, but for those that are, it can be revealing to plot the work in progress of a programme or portfolio against the services and service stages it relates to. You can compare work against the service performance criteria discussed in chapter 3 to help direct and steer it, or you could share the whole service context with the teams delivering the change using chapter 2 to build a shared view. This process can also reveal the gaps in the work being done. If these gaps correspond with known problems, that's a valuable conversation to have with senior leadership.

What makes it hard and what to do about it

It's not a straightforward task to change the direction and how progress is assessed for a major programme. Even if you are the person in charge, there will be many influences that are outside your direct control.

Here are three common barriers and a few ways to try to work through or around them.

The timing
It's difficult to bring about major change out of the blue. It suggests the logic was faulty to begin with, which can be hard to convince some people of (and to acknowledge) without new evidence.

If there's already a shared sense that things need to change, you can collectively position it as an important 'evolution' that stands on the shoulders of what came before.

You could wait for a major event and introduce changes off the back of it: a major reduction in expected funding, for example, or a replanning exercise, a sudden change in major priorities, or a challenge from external governance or audit processes.

Alternatively, you can begin the slower process of challenging how likely it is that the current approach and trajectory will achieve the right goals or solve the known problems. Rather than being a harbinger of doom (which anyone can do), you'll have greater impact if you can provide a sensible and attractive alternative: either a better approach or a framework that supports more substantive assessment and new thinking about the current activity.

Negotiating commitments

In public service, political commitments can set the agenda for what is delivered. When commitments are made that set out a roadmap or timelines for particular work, it can inspire – but it can also constrain. This is risky when it's based on a false certainty that hasn't been well handled.

Not all commitments are the same. Knowing exactly what has been committed to can reveal where there is flexibility. Some commitments are internal and can be moved. Some are public, but only in terms of a few politicians or leaders having expectations that could evolve with the right data. Other commitments are made very publicly, or are part of a political manifesto or corporate plan, which makes them harder to change. If there are really good reasons, though, it is still possible. The sooner people know about the need to change or adjust commitments, the better the chances of doing something about it.

The wording of commitments is critical. Ideally, build in flexibility to ensure there's space to learn and iterate the approach to achieve the desired outcomes. Don't let announcements happen without scrutinizing every word. Make sure a commitment doesn't run counter to the approaches and methods that will help the organization learn and adapt to deliver something sensible.

Dealing with resistance

Sometimes, people are certain about uncertain things and that's that. Not everyone will be interested in your experience or observation that false certainty isn't an acceptable position, especially where taxpayers or shareholders are concerned. Folks can misunderstand or misrepresent what you're saying. For example, they might accuse you of pushing for an unachievable 'gold standard', or say that whatever you're suggesting 'won't work here' or that it's 'too late'.

In this situation you might have a better chance of sensible discussions with different people. But it's worth putting the effort in to first understand existing concerns people have in general about the programme or portfolio. It's unusual for nobody to be concerned when large amounts of money are involved. See if you can help draw together something that points towards the issues and leads to a better answer – or, at least, to constructive challenge and robust conversation. Leaders in positions of scrutiny and accountability will be thankful for well-constructed analysis and evidence that illuminates any points of weakness or blind spots they can raise.

Summary

① Set out the overall vision, goals and objective success criteria – and relate them to the corresponding teams and projects – to steer the work in a portfolio towards outcomes, or to see where to make changes if the connection isn't strong enough.

② Teams as well as domain experts should assess and track work in progress using criteria that include strategy and direction, external impact on customers and users, the implications for the organization and the operation, whether it leads to capability building, and the approach and deliverability of the work.

③ Write clear descriptions of all the work involved in order to shine a light on which parts are self-evidently needed and which parts have a murkier rationale.

④ Map the work to services, and use the service performance framework to assess and steer it where appropriate.

⑤ Barriers to change include timing and prior commitments. Yet there can still be ways to influence the direction if you can make a compelling logical case backed by evidence that it's worthwhile.

Moving to outcomes-based governance
Citizens Advice

Citizens Advice provides confidential information and advice to assist people with legal, debt, consumer, benefits, housing and other problems in the UK.

Services are supported by 'internal products', such as case management, contact centre platforms and other tools to support referrals to external organizations. Kylie Havelock is their head of product. Kylie joined in January 2019 and has introduced an approach to delivering these products that's iterative. This has required evolving the traditional governance, which wasn't set up for modern product development that is ongoing.

Kylie and her team have been evolving the process to focus the work on outcomes – and to align it with overall strategy. They began by identifying the single most important priority that internal products could influence. For Citizens Advice, this was 'advisor efficiency'. For them, that means figuring out what will help more customers in the same amount of time or what will more easily solve complex customer needs. By understanding what's driving the work, teams can identify achievable outcomes and metrics that support it, and they can establish targets that give a sense of progress.

As one example, 'no-show appointments' result in lost advisor time. A product team might test out different ideas – sending a reminder text message, for example, or designing clearer booking confirmation – to reduce no shows, quantifying the impact. If there is evidence that reminder text messages perform best, the team might build this feature in and agree a target of 5% reduction in no shows within 12 months. This helps them to assess progress, to know it's worth it, and to learn what gets in the way.

Outcomes, metrics and targets now provide a view of the current work by product teams, as well as what's planned. Teams use a scoring system of 1–4 to assess how on track they are to deliver agreed outcomes, adding what they've learned or how they've iterated to improve progress. A product board meets monthly to discuss progress and how to support teams to remove blockers and maximize their impact. Kylie explains:[6]

> We needed to work together to grow our own understanding and capability first, before attempting to apply outcomes-based working wholesale. We've had great feedback from stakeholders, who are much better informed about what we're doing, what's important and what we've achieved. We've also been supporting a wider cultural move towards outcomes-based approaches in the rest of the organization – for example, as part of our annual budgeting process – by sharing our work in the open, to provide a useful case study in how to apply this type of approach in practice.

Spotting the gaps in a large portfolio

One large organization made a significant investment in a new system for caseworkers. The goal was to reduce bottlenecks by automating some of the tasks, and to improve consistency in decision making by providing better tools for checks and validation for staff. Mapping all of the work taking place across the whole service revealed that no improvements were being made to the 'start', however – that is, to the content and guidance that signposted users to apply for the service. And yet some of the bottlenecks in casework were caused by people applying for the wrong service for their situation. A small team set up two quick experiments to give an indication of the size of the opportunity. They invited a sample of research participants to read the guidance and then choose which service they would apply for. They then asked them to rate how confident they were that they had made the right choice. Most people picked the wrong option, and yet were confident they'd made the right choice. This evidence of avoidable effort formed the business case to create tools to guide people to make the right choices in the first place – not just the technology used in subsequent decision making.

Chapter 11

Revolutionize governance for services

Governance is less about going to the right boards and more about supporting flow of (the right) work and decision making. But the bigger prize is to embed the culture, standards, decision-making authority and working practice to create better services by default.

Figuring out how governance worked in a given organization used to feel tedious to me. At the time, I couldn't see how the processes contributed, or how they changed what teams were doing to deliver anything. It felt like hoops to jump through to get something done, not something that resulted in more valuable or joined-up work.

But when there's a lot happening at different levels across an organization, there are many different types of decisions and choices that need to be made: the type of work, the approach, rework or reuse, design or policy options, choices of tech, the level or type of investment, standards to use or support models. Who makes or 'approves' these decisions, how well they understand the detail and context, and how familiar they are with modern ways of working determine the success. So if you aren't involved in 'governance', you can miss opportunities to influence services at scale. Maintaining the quality and flow of work and decision making requires trust between teams. In practice, this means that people need to know what's going on, the direction things are moving in, and the rationale for this, and be able to intervene or argue for something different.

That said, the governance goal is for decision making and guidance to happen *at an appropriate level*. One that's grounded in context and reality, and not just in ideals, power structures or naivety. Good service governance means asking: What should teams involved in the work be able to decide for themselves on the basis that they're closest to what's realistic or what's actually happening? What makes sense to look at across many teams or by people outside the team? What are universal principles (rather than hard 'rules') to be guided by? These are all good service governance questions. It's when governance is wrongly applied, focuses on the wrong things or is forced into the wrong role that it becomes frustrating.

'Governance' typically refers to the processes and means that organizations use to exert control over the delivery of work, as well as its value. This chapter is about how to influence and organize governance processes and culture towards better services. This isn't about establishing a(nother) new authority for others to present to – although in some situations that can be a necessary first step. The bigger prize is to embed the outside-in service mindset, alongside the teams, leadership, ways of working and delivery approaches, so that the work we invest in improves the services it affects, by default, without the need for the oversight of dozens of boards, working groups, authorities and committees. True service organizations don't need to follow the same traditions as older institutions. When you work in modern ways to begin with, there's much you can remove from the original process. This is a profound cultural shift for many organizations.

Name the issues

Healthy governance requires that people and processes can deliver fast, 'good enough' decisions, using evidence, expertise and recent experience, while anticipating the need and creating opportunities for deeper challenge and scrutiny where necessary.

Corporate boards have specific legal and financial responsibilities and accountabilities determined by their industry and location. But there are countless other groups that have influence over the success of work: (sub) boards, committees, assurance groups, authorities and working groups. Their remit and focus is more a result of the individuals involved and the 'terms of reference' that have been agreed.

And there are typical ways in which governance processes at these levels don't do what folks assume or trust they do. Rarely does anyone quantify the time and effort an organization invests in each governance action or decision, let alone whether the quality of decision making increases or even reduces as a result.

Here are a few examples of when governance processes don't do what people might believe they do.

1. When it's more about stakeholder engagement and communication than it is about high-quality scrutiny and decision making. Signs of this include too many people being involved, it being hard to get consent or consensus, boundaries being unclear, new people turning up or filling in for others frequently, doing more questioning than decision making.

2. When there's a very large number of different governance forums. Organizations typically add layers of governance rather than remove them, but this is the wrong answer to many of the underlying problems. They can stall progress altogether if they give overlapping or conflicting advice if

leaders aren't looking at how governance works overall or at what's needed.

3. When experiences and skills are missing or when there's over-representation of one agenda or set of beliefs. There's often a lack of representation of those with recent or current experience of operations, of users, and of modern delivery and digital approaches. The analysis and the options presented can include inbuilt bias or hidden risk, which wouldn't be obvious to busy folk in scrutinizing roles. Allies can be missing who would otherwise provide the challenge or support to direct work to measurably improve services.

4. When the process bakes in the need to 'know' or predict all the answers up front. This involves demanding increasingly detailed but speculative slides and reassurances about work that hasn't even started, as well as other unhelpful steers that run counter to being able to learn about reality and iterate.

5. Where teams are inhibited or prevented from making decisions or steering direction for themselves for the situations where they are best placed to safely do so. This is where even low-level decisions get bottlenecked and 'stuck', or where there's simply a lack of clarity as to what or who is needed to definitively decide or approve a course of action.

It doesn't always matter. There are plenty of people who are skilled at navigating large organizations, making good things happen despite plenty of less-than-ideal working practice.

But start by giving a name to the issues that you see, and then look for the opportunities – and the right timing – to address them. Make observations in conversation. Get involved in work to adjust or overhaul how governance works. Invite others who are missing. Or turn the points above into positive principles to overhaul, establish or improve processes.

Shape the process for work to start, stop or continue

At scale, there are benefits to codifying how 'work' flows or progresses from an initial idea. One way to do this is by forming official phases of work from start to live operations. Funnelling work through a lifecycle like this creates opportunities to

- shape the work that is a priority into the right way to deliver it, involving the expertise needed to do this well;
- assess how work should be approached, what to consider, and what constitutes success;
- stop projects that won't work, aren't worthwhile or aren't as important right now;
- point to a process as a way to set expectations and to push back or negotiate requests to start more pieces of work; and
- have inbuilt points of intervention to keep – or get – things on the right path and to assess progress.

The UK's Government Digital Service set out an agile lifecycle[1] that puts the emphasis on learning and delivering value by 'doing', and it has since been copied and adapted by countries and organizations all over the world. A version of this is probably already happening in the organization you work with. It just won't necessarily be designed or used to join up work, set outcomes, improve service performance or involve people with recent experience of operations, of users or of modern ways of working for delivery. Use the following seven phases as inspiration to consider what happens with the organization you work with and what could be improved. Develop a version that will encourage the right behaviours for your context. Not all stages that follow will apply to all situations. It partly depends on the experience, expertise and alignment of those involved, as well as the type of work. The goal is to get to the most streamlined version of this that is possible while still upholding the principles of each phase. You could mandate a process like this at first, later evolving to allow greater flexibility.

Figure 11. Shape how work flows through an organization.

1. Triaging new ideas or requests

New ideas or requests come from many different sources, which makes it hard to prevent the progression of ideas that aren't a priority or aren't well aligned or shaped.

One solution is to funnel all requests and ideas through one single, consistent process. This will help you take control and be in a position to shape work for success. Establishing a single process for all new work requests and ideas results in a single view, which allows for more cohesive assessment of ideas. Some work has a force multiplier effect on the teams that are aligned to priorities, even if it doesn't sound like a priority in and of itself. By funnelling all ideas into one process, you're better able to gather together the right people to assess the opportunity or value.

When new ideas arise through the life cycle and from ongoing operations, it's a good idea to repeat a similar assessment process to compare these opportunities against other priorities.

2. Assessing potential

Some rapid analysis can help everyone better understand the nature of the request or the problem to solve. The idea is to understand whether a piece of work is worth it, by clarifying

- the goals and rationale;
- how important it could be in the grand scheme of things;
- where and how it might fit;
- the level of uncertainty, risk or potential impact;
- the likely complexity (that may not be visible to others initially); and, importantly,
- whether to do anything about it at all.

This needs to be high level and low effort. It's to avoid the need to establish a larger team if the work isn't a priority, isn't feasible or can be addressed in another way. Include input from the people involved in service delivery, design and improvement.

Try asking the following questions.

- What does this mean for users? What is it that we present externally that people have to understand, do or interact with? How does it relate to the services the organization provides or to individual steps within them?
- Do we – or how do we – know this will work? Or know it's likely to be good? What is the evidence for it? Have we prototyped and tested it with real users, for example? Does someone need to go away and find out more first?
- What are the possible problems with it?
- What criteria would we use to evaluate it?

These questions are easy to answer if a team has undergone a good discovery or problem-exploration activity. They're intentionally hard for those who have jumped to one upfront solution without a compelling rationale. And it's also a quick way to judge how much this matters.

Possible decisions at this stage include recommending the work continue to the next phase, stopping it there, suggesting it is handled as part of something else, or storing the idea for a future date.

3. Setting direction or strategy, and designing policy

The overall direction, policy or strategy is naturally going to continue to change as learning continues throughout all phases. But this stage allows for some deeper exploration of goals, options and logic to assess if it's still worth progressing.

At this stage, no one should dictate how something might be delivered later. The goal is to protect the time and space required for genuinely multidisciplinary teams to learn how best to do this themselves. But what this stage does is to determine, or to rule out, some of the potential options, as well as to consider how to prioritize given resource constraints.

This still needs to be relatively low effort, before larger teams get involved. Be sure to include input from people who are close to potential users, as well as those who are familiar with how delivery teams work.

Expectations need to be set that the proposed work won't necessarily be taken forward after this point. In fact, from this point onwards, everything needs to be ruthlessly prioritized because spend dramatically increases through the need to establish larger, focused teams.

4. Explore

This is a time-limited phase to establish a multidisciplinary team to learn much more about an opportunity or a problem to solve, the context, and the potential value. In the UK government service manual, this phase is called 'discovery'.[2] It includes who the users are and what's needed, analysis for understanding potential value, the investment situation and the possible risks. It makes recommendations for what to do next.

The team that does this exploration should be the same team that will take the work forwards, as far as possible. But the work isn't guaranteed to continue past this point, because what's uncovered could be a good reason to stop further work that doesn't match the vision or priorities – or isn't going to work or be deliverable. And to continue, the case needs to be clear that it's more worthwhile to carry on working in this space than it would be to give attention to anything else.

Given the complexity alongside all the other work often in play, people with big-picture vision – as well as an understanding of the current landscape – are needed to help guide the approach: connecting the dots to see how to reduce fragmentation or to figure out sensible ways to learn about and deliver change across complicated portfolios of existing teams. If a brand new team undertakes this work without situational context, there's a greater risk of discovering 'things we already know' or of making recommendations that don't 'fit' – or don't challenge – what else is already underway. Blend new teams with those who understand the context and landscape, or make them available on the periphery to a 'core' team. Chapter 4 includes guidelines for how to shape work for success.

If there is significant pressure from influential parties to do something that isn't aligned to the strategy or priorities – and that can't be batted away by other means – an 'explore' phase such as this can provide the evidence needed to support the negotiation and handling of the situation.

To retain control over portfolios, next steps could include letting the work continue or identifying what it should replace; stopping it or merging it with something else; or putting it on the pile for another time.

5. Learn, test, build, change or implement – and iterate
These phases are to test and learn which options will work best, and if it is appropriate to then adopt the best approach and scale or improve it. Teams can still uncover reasons to stop work

at this stage, or to delay it until later. For example, if it's dependent on data being available that isn't, it might not be possible or worth the effort.

Teams will be learning and gathering evidence about

- what's needed;
- how to design, build or implement;
- how best to address the risks;
- how to operate;
- what's needed to safely scale it;
- what will make it as good as possible given the constraints; and
- what's worth investing in to improve it further.

Service leadership and coordination are important to choreograph change and improvement across the whole (see chapters 7 and 9). Use service views and measurement (see chapters 2 and 3) to help prioritize where it's worth investing in improvement or ways to scale. Chapter 10 gives examples of specific criteria to use to run a regular assessment process throughout, which you can use to evaluate standards being used and choices that may impact other teams.

Decision points include continuing to grow, intervening to change it or find out more, going back a few steps to reassess potential, or winding down and stopping work.

6. Operate and improve

This is ongoing activity to operate, maintain and improve services, as well as the individual components that support them. For whole services this includes all the behind-the-scenes and frontline activity and processes. For supporting capabilities it includes the ongoing running and improving of tools, products, platforms and other technology.

Rather than this being a 'handoff to business as usual', it represents a shift in the focus and make-up of teams. The focus is more likely on scale and growth, managing demand, improving performance, efficiency or security. The make-up of teams might shift to incorporate service monitoring, account management or customer support, for example.

For extensive changes to a live service, or for complex pieces of work that affect services, the cycle of phases may need to repeat, so that all potential work is considered against overall priorities.

7. Wind down

This is the work to safely end, migrate, transition and close down what is no longer needed or has reached the end of its term.

*

Teams need the flexibility to take a step back and rethink any of these phases based on the evidence being generated. It's a life cycle that aims to embed learning more about the risks at an early stage, as well as controlling the direction and volume of work.

Some people would be concerned that a process like this would work against the principle of having empowered teams that make their own decisions. They would want to shape and scope work to remove or reduce any dependencies, so that teams aren't 'held up'. It is possible to isolate some kinds of work in this way, but it isn't realistic for every type of work or team in a large organization or for a large service.

Other people worry that a process like this takes time. But it's not the process that adds the time. It's deciding what's worth finding out at the start that dictates the time. The longer it takes to uncover and tackle the issues that have a material impact on risk, cost or success factors, the harder it is to unpick and resteer – unless the delivery approach has been designed to avoid this. In some cases it pushes back the start of what *looks* like delivery, but only to avoid the problem of having a large team in place to then find out we're not doing the right thing. It's a way to protect investment and make sure the higher-performing pieces of work are prioritized.

If you find that work in these early stages isn't so valuable, we're not learning quickly enough, it's overly specified, or if it's assumed that the work will proceed regardless of what we find out, change what's allowed into this process, as well as how it's done. You may need to gather allies and collectively (and frequently) reset expectations. It's the principles that are important, not the process itself.

Control how new work starts

Controlling the pipeline of work is vital to protect the time and space needed to do the most important work well enough. Parts of the organization are always likely to push forward ideas that seem overconfident, aren't aligned with strategy, or that are pet projects that don't improve anything overall.

Control can mean being able to say no. Or doing some analysis to provide evidence for why something shouldn't be done. It could mean reshaping the piece of work, or figuring out an alternative approach that might mean it gets delayed for the good of overall strategy and deliverability.

If teams can't control – or at least heavily influence – the new work being initiated, it's also incredibly hard to change other habits. The more work in progress there is, the harder it is for leadership and influencers to find the time, or learn, or introduce different ways of working for anyone else.

What follows are ideas that other services and organizations have used to give this process the right powers.

A team that acts as a gatekeeper
Some organizations have established a team that knows enough about how existing services work to more safely anticipate how other pieces of work will affect them – and that also understands the strategy or policy very well. They have the

skills to work closely with executives, politicians, finance and policy leads.

They're available to talk to the rest of the organization (or wherever ideas come from) and to intercept incoming requests for teams or for changes to services, programmes or portfolios. Of course the people involved need to understand this isn't a process for the sake of it, and they must be prepared to do everything possible to support ideas that are straightforward, sensible or a priority. There's a distinction between proposals from high-performing teams or individuals with good domain and contextual understanding who understand the trade-offs, and situations where the value, urgency or situational awareness is much more doubtful.

It needs people who are skilled in negotiation and diplomacy who can work well with other functions, lobbying groups, policy teams or executives. Their remit is to protect the priorities and also to protect everyone else who is working to deliver them. Based on knowledge and, importantly, evidence, they can develop well-argued responses to requests or pressure to do something. A team like this can save an organization significant time and effort later.

Some organizations will empower these teams to turn down work, although this puts them in an unenviable position in the face of pressure from senior leaders. An alternative is to recommend saying no and explain why. Because of a lack of confidence in the idea, for example, or because of the level of risk and complexity. Because of the likely drag on other priorities or the lack of availability of teams. This leaves the ultimate decision to whoever is accountable.

But then the accountable person has to be someone who deeply feels the downside of proceeding anyway – such as the cost, technical debt, or doing something that doesn't work for users – while having equal power with those pushing for the idea. So, for example, a single function of the organization (finance, policy, marketing, legal) can't push through decisions without regard for the impact on everything else just to satisfy those that they in turn feel pressure from.

This approach isn't without problems. It's a coping mechanism in the face of conflicting or otherwise-unmanageable pressure, when the ideal might be that teams closest to 'the work' have their own processes to agree and prioritize what happens. Inevitably, a gatekeeping team like this could become a bottleneck, be biased towards (or against) one kind of work over another, or be expected to have the same level of domain expertise that only a specialist team in that area will have. The team's effectiveness rests on everyone understanding the level of change the organization has capacity for, the right disciplines and specialists being involved, some consistency of analysis, and a fallback or escalation process.

Some organizations have created an alternative delivery approach that allows them to 'outsource' ideas that are less obviously 'core' to the organization, less valuable or not widely supported – but that need to happen anyway, for various unavoidable reasons. This means either having a separate specialist team inside the organization to work on novel ideas or using external suppliers. Doing this can protect the more permanent domain-experienced teams and keep them doing the most valuable and strategic work, which keeps valuable knowledge and capability in-house.

Investigators and translators

With experience you can anticipate some of the problems that a piece of work might cause, or encounter, but in some cases it's hard to negotiate without knowing more or having evidence. Making one or two trusted people available with real depth of knowledge and experience in a few key areas is invaluable.

These are 'investigators' who can spend time with a team, or actively seek out potentially critical problems, and share a concise overview. They act as a critical friend to the teams themselves, helping them to shape the best approach.

Comparisons

One useful aid to discussion is to compare new ideas against each other in terms of their potential value or impact. Nominate one person to objectively present the rationale for why something is a good idea. Facilitate a discussion (among peers, leadership or decision makers) to deconstruct ideas into component parts and collectively weigh them up against what else could be achieved with the same time and effort.

Objective(ish) scoring criteria

Some organizations use scoring criteria to arrive at more nuanced analysis that helps them prioritize and steer work more objectively. It provides a foundation for decisions about work that leaves an audit trail. Consider impact for customers and users, deliverability, organizational or policy goals, operations, technology, security or data, and whether the work helps to develop important capability or moves the organization towards modern ways of working.

Setting limits

When there is a serious overall risk to deliverability or success for a programme or portfolio, the right thing can be to freeze all new work for a period of time, or have a 'one in, one out' rule. This is to allow senior leaders and seasoned experts to focus on what's most important or urgent when there are capacity issues. But it requires a great deal of trust to be able to do this.

Setting limits on work in progress can be a critical part of protecting time and space. Some organizations put limits on the number of pieces of work that can be in any of these phases at any one time, simply saying 'No, we're full' to any more. But since pieces of work can be bundled up or fragmented to get around this, a way to size the effort is needed too.

Gather people together for substantive discussion

One exercise some modern organizations use is to have people write a short outline of an idea to gather critical challenge and feedback rapidly before further effort is made. It's a valuable process for well-thought-through ideas, as well as a way of spotting the poorly articulated requests.

- Write a short (one- or two-page) document outlining an idea (there are ideas in chapters 4 and 6 for prompts to use).
- Read together as a group for 10–20 minutes, individually adding notes and thoughts to the document.
- Host substantive discussion for 40 minutes.

The group will make more progress in an hour than is possible in any amount of time spent trying to separately interpret and send feedback to the team.

How to negotiate
When faced with pressure to do work that doesn't seem likely to be successful, find ways to build in some flexibility.

- How much is within the remit of the organization, programme, portfolio, leadership or team alone to decide? How much involves upwards and outwards negotiation, analysis and recommendation?
- For issues around deliverability in the face of commitments, how much flexibility is there in the definition or exact wording of those commitments? Who was the commitment made with? Was it internal or external? If it was with boards or executives or politicians, is it already public?
- Does the work in question get in the way of what we're trying to achieve? Can it go ahead but in a way that doesn't cause other problems for now? Will it have a damaging impact on something else important?
- Does it break with good service or delivery principles or standards?

There are nearly always ways of managing the situation. Don't just tell influential people that they're asking the wrong question or are proposing the wrong idea: provide a better question or a better, safer idea that addresses some of the underlying motives. Alternatively, point out what won't happen if what they are asking for goes ahead, to check they're aware of the implications and risks.

Challenge how it works today

This chapter has focused so far on governance of the flow of work and of creating opportunities to intercept and influence work at different stages. But there will be many other governance processes that influence the direction and value of work.

Know the existing governance process
Traditionally managed portfolios can have incredibly complicated governance. I've seen diagrams attempting to map 'governance' that are the size of a billboard. Elsewhere, I've seen people spend six months mapping the governance and still not feel they have an exhaustive view.

Large organizations have similar (sounding) governance forums. You'll find labels such as the design authority, the business design authority, the technical design authority, transformation boards, and programme and portfolio boards. Each will have terms of reference that set out what they influence or make decisions about.

Follow the journey of a few different pieces of work to find out how many steps there are, how many authorities or forums thought they should be involved and about what, and how long it took teams to do what was required. Build a rough working model of what's going on, what works and what doesn't. This can be incredibly eye-opening to senior leaders and executives and can open up the opportunity to improve.

Identify the right people to work with
Changing (or evolving) the governance approach requires working with leadership and relevant governance leads, as well as

those that give authority to spend. Get to know the people that you can work alongside to improve governance. A good, modern project management office (PMO) function or individuals from that team can help address the challenges. More traditional PMO approaches don't always fit comfortably with the principle of enabling teams to learn and iterate, or they can even work to thwart the working practices and trust that are needed. It can come down to the culture, behaviours and attitudes on all sides.

A good start is to find one other leader who shares the same concerns about risk management and governance processes. You can be a great ally in helping them to make significant improvements and to challenge current processes across the organization.

Point out the risks
Healthy governance should have inbuilt mechanisms that enforce and protect – and don't inhibit – good working practice and early learning about risks.

Here are a few reasonable challenges that governance can either support or get in the way of.

- Does the governance process put appropriate decision making in the hands of the teams closest to, or actually doing, the work, as far as is humanly possible (i.e. does it support autonomy of teams)? Is it clear what kinds of decision are best made at different levels and who has authority for what? If not, there should be a mandate to develop a clearer model.
- Does the governance process challenge people to work in modern ways that involve testing, learning and iterating to gather evidence? Or does it inhibit it?
- Does it undermine the quality of what we're delivering or what it is that we're trying to achieve overall? Either because it's about outputs rather than outcomes, or because it doesn't address the hidden risks.
- Does it help and prompt people to provide proper challenge and scrutiny, over both what we do and how we do it, i.e. how

we start work, how we assess performance and progress, and how we establish teams?

- Does it include the right people across disciplines in order to provide robust challenge to decisions? Make sure a blend of people and skill sets are invited to join key forums. Identify where there are gaps in diverse-enough representation at those forums.

Drum up support for change by developing a short, convincing and logical argument about what needs to be addressed and how, working with other allies and governance leads to do so, and present this collective view to leadership.

Boards and accountability

It's the duty of members of the corporate board and of executives to bring scrutiny, critical challenge and external accountability. But if individual board members aren't seeing the right data or are not at the right level of detail, it will be hard for them to fulfil this responsibility.

Individuals should welcome information and details that help them bring effective challenge. In fact, they can and should seek it out by circulating around the organization. Talk to people internally to find out who engages with board members. Find the people in positions of scrutiny whose background is closest to what it takes to make good products and services. Increasingly, boards will have at least one individual with a 'digital' background. These people benefit from knowing people and roles within the organization who can help them to help the rest of the board form more balanced views of the risks and opportunities.

Summary

① Get to know how the governance works by following a few pieces of work through the process. Develop a model to show what works and what doesn't, including the missed opportunities to improve service performance.

② Find and work with others to develop opportunities to evolve governance processes and to present a more powerful, collective argument for change.

③ Codify what should and should not happen across the whole life cycle of work, from new idea or request through to live operation and improvement.

④ Include people in governance processes who can provide insights and challenge based on the reality of operations, of customers and users, of technology and of policy – and who understand modern ways of working in multidisciplinary teams.

⑤ Establish controls over how new work starts in order to protect priorities, and to create the opportunity to set work up for success or to improve its impact on services.

⑥ The need for some governance forums and processes will reduce and evolve as more of the organization adopts modern ways of working that build in the ability to learn and course-correct, allowing decision making and direction to move closer to the work in hand.

Service governance includes day-to-day operations as well as larger, strategic change
HM Passport Office, UK
HM Passport Office is the issuer of UK passports and responsible for civil registration services in England & Wales through the General Register Office.

Colin Foley, head of business and service design, explains how governance processes have evolved as HM Passport Office becomes a service organization.[3]

Originally we had many different working groups. We had already moved towards a smaller number of 'mission boards' to focus on what we wanted to achieve in terms of our transformation and strategic goals. That worked well, but what we were transforming to was a service business. For that, we needed a service board that understands and represents the whole. It couldn't be separated from operations.

The service governance we have now looks at overall service performance, the insight and intel that's coming in, and the important topics that affect performance day to day, such as finance, pain points, supplier and commercial arrangements. An additional board focuses on supporting and guiding what is changing across the service: the work that we do to try to reach our service goals, how we understand the change that's happening, and what we expect in terms of performance improvements or other strategic benefits. There's a balance of short-term and longer-term changes underway.

Decisions are intended to be based on service data and evidence wherever possible; not solely opinions. We look at what's needed and compare that with what's planned. If important service issues aren't going to be addressed by what's already there, we'll feed new requests into budget planning and business cases.

A 'quartet' of people (an operational service manager, a digital service owner, a business architect or a service designer, and a technical architect) work together to govern and prioritize the overarching service backlog and to keep that forward look. That helps them to do the prioritization for individual product roadmaps and gives digital service teams the insight to choose the right work to do.

Bring new perspectives to existing governance forums
The Home Office, UK
The Home Office is the UK government department responsible for immigration, security, law and order. The Home Office Business Design Authority (BDA) is responsible for the significant

design decisions that affect services. The strategy and change directors that make up the board saw the opportunity to evolve this forum to better reflect strategy and priorities across the department rather than at local business area levels, as well as to further embed insight from operations, user-centred design and policy.

Katy Arnold is the former deputy director of experience and strategy delivery within Home Office Digital, Data and Technology. Working with the new chair of the BDA, Katy facilitated interviews with board members across the organization to understand what was and was not working. The board had a set of design principles giving some parameters for decision-making, but they had become outdated. Katy established a small multidisciplinary working group to bring these principles up to date. She explains:[4]

> I spent time getting to know individuals across different professions, to develop a mutually shared view of what was needed, and to establish that this was a opportunity for us to genuinely work together to strengthen the principles and improve governance by including what was missing in decision-making, while reinforcing the role of the organization as a service provider. We were able to incorporate important points, such as shaping investment to improve or join up services, gathering evidence about the impact on people involved – our external and internal users – and designing for greater trust and inclusion.
>
> The working group included user-centred designers, business designers, data architects and content designers. We got to know individual design authority boards and strategy teams across the organization to start to align what they were doing. This gave us a useful perspective of everything that was happening, which meant we could bring in the strategic direction of the organization to our other work.
>
> These principles are now used for every programme or major project that comes to the board. Teams need to show that they're undertaking appropriate activity to understand their users and

others affected, and they are including a test-and-learn approach with users during design and build, ensuring people are considered across the whole. All of this needs to happen before seeking financial approval at the department's investment committee.

Prioritization across a large service
DWP, Universal Credit, UK
Deb Boore, transformation and delivery director, Universal Credit, DWP, shares how planning and governance works for a very large, live service.[5]

We manage our design in six-month phases. We determine the initial priorities as a multidisciplinary team: what do we think we can fit in, what's most important, what will help us be more efficient or help customers do the right things? Then we make other calls on priorities. Things that are legislative and have fixed dates, or that bring operational efficiencies – it can't just make life 'easier', it has to have a value and impact. And of course we involve others across the department at this stage, particularly colleagues with responsibility for policy and fraud.

We then take these major prioritization decisions through a number of working groups and design authorities before endorsement by formal programme governance.

Each feature team is then in control of prioritizing their own activity within the phase, which is critical in terms of empowerment and responsiveness. These teams comprise business analysts, operational experts, developers, testers, user researchers and designers. They'll decide their approach and in what order they do things.

Alongside regular prioritization, we'll do a mid-phase review of progress, also considering whether the things we prioritized three months ago are still the most important to us.

And of course, given the scale of the Universal Credit service now, we need to impact a wide range of policy changes and new initiatives that could affect how the service operates. We do this at a working level so that the whole range of impacts are clear and we have sufficient data to decide our response. This means that we often have to turn down requests for changes to Universal Credit where our existing priorities will deliver greater value to the organization.

Governance as an enabler
DfE, England: Teacher Services

The Department for Education (DfE) is responsible for children's services and education, including early years, schools, higher and further education policy, apprenticeships and wider skills in England.

The DfE is also responsible for teaching. This includes who teaches, teaching standards and what gets taught. They provide services to teachers, including supporting people to become teachers.

Rachel Hope is the former service owner for Teacher Services and Pete Ward is the current deputy director. They describe how an *enabling team* has become an important part of the governance process and is critical to being able to deliver at pace.[6]

Rather than a traditional Project Management Office (PMO) we have an enabling team. It means there is someone there to work on any finance, commercial or people risks or issues that come up through the course of delivery, on behalf of everyone. Whether they are policy designers or product managers. If the PMO is only about tracking and reporting as a form of assurance, rather than solving, you just can't move quickly enough. We tried hard to avoid all the usual reporting processes that don't actually result in the bigger risks being addressed and dealt with. Having the enabling team means they can directly tackle what gets in the way and we couldn't have achieved what we have without them. It's an entirely different approach to risk which requires a change in mindset from everyone involved. Delivery teams often see governance as something to avoid, whilst reporting functions may mistrust agile teams for not having the sorts of roadmaps they're used to. Offering delivery teams additional help, and bringing people closer to the reality of the challenges, means everyone is better prepared, but peo- ple often need to experience it before they're able to fully get the difference.

Giving teams and work the best chance of success
Establishing a 'triage and assess' capability for new work
It's not uncommon for a very large organization to have dozens of 'requests' for work and investment in new projects or teams each month. How do you decide what's feasible or most needed, on a case-by-case basis, like this?

Matti Keltanen is an expert in service organizations. He shares a practical way to review a large number of ideas, by creating a triage and assessment capability, most recently adopted by a large UK government department. He explains:

Ideas for 'new work' come from many directions: leadership, product or service teams, customers or user research, or externally (regulators, lobbyists, other stakeholders). When dealing with a large volume of requests, you can't afford to do a deep dive to better understand each one. So the first step is to take stock of all the new pieces of work and requests currently in play, to then establish a triage process to screen out which of these are clear and straightforward.

This leaves a smaller set of more 'involved' requests. One way I've found that works to assess these is to bring together different experts (including those with skills not normally found in traditional governance processes, such as product, user research, or technology and security) to give their views on potential risks or complexities they recognize in their area of expertise, discussing it with those who 'own' or are working on the idea. They might meet weekly to discuss all the incoming ideas and to select the one or two to do a deeper dive on, gathering again to form a combined view of recommendations. They can also advise teams about the kind of expertise and individuals they might need, which won't necessarily be obvious to those that haven't worked with 'digital capability' on a team before.

The individuals involved need hands-on understanding of their areas to do this well. For example, to analyse the potential impact on the organization's customers or users you need to know the reality of the existing users and how they interact with the organization's products or services. To look at technical feasibility or other impacts on the technical landscape, you should know the current technology stack or architecture, as well as modern technology practice and so on. You may also need to involve people who understand competition, the regulatory environment or other external constraints, as well as those who know the organization and its workings well – how to navigate it, the power and information structures, and what other initiatives are going on that could be related.

Having a checklist helps a group like this to analyse opportunities consistently. It could cover the following.

- Is there a clear reason to do this? Is there a clear problem and a sensible approach to it? Does it make sense for the organization to do this?
- What are the big unknowns or risks at this point? Where are there potential but non-obvious pitfalls? These are often in domains where only special expertise can identify the level of complexity or risk involved, e.g. impact on users, or technology, or legislation/policy, or security. An early 'heads up' from a deep domain expert will be vital for any team taking on a piece of work.
- Who is needed to work on it? Identify the key skills and expertise needed. But protect a team from overcrowding

- don't include everyone in a core team, instead offering broader support around a smaller core set of people.
- Can we and should we take this on? Is there capacity without trying to do too many things at once? Is it too tangled up with other work that needs unpacking before this gets anywhere near starting? What should be the focus or likely be done first?
- How should this be approached? Does this need more information before anything else? For example, a 'discovery' phase, careful planning, quick prototypes to learn something more, or something else?

Forming a collective view is a powerful basis for constructively challenging requests, as well as setting up the right support and conditions for high-performing teams. It may turn out that an idea should be turned down, changed or addressed later on – in which case a well-argued and well-rounded basis for doing so is exactly what leadership needs to intervene.

Chapter 12

Win support from people at the top

Asking for something is a good way to learn how much the person you're talking to is in a position to be able to support you.

To make better service organizations in a way that is sustainable, you'll need support and cover from senior leaders. Use this chapter to help you set out how to address the important challenges organizations already want to solve.

In large organizations, ideas are often shared through slide decks. You can use this chapter to prepare a slide deck, a talk or prompts for a conversation. Divide things up into three sections: the problem, the solution and next steps. Finish by asking your audience for something. There are excellent guides that go into more detail about how to communicate well at this level.[1]

Start with the important problems

Start with what the person or group you're talking to cares about. All large organizations have problems. Many are known but others are more hidden, obvious only once you've called them out. Your organization will have both. For example:

- Teams solve the same problem multiple times.
- We don't arrive at the best option for the problems.
- Time is wasted developing poor solutions, and then more time is lost unpicking them.
- Time is wasted in meetings when the thinking, language, evidence or rationale isn't clear.
- We don't organize or design in a way that matches what users expect, need or want to do, resulting in friction, pain, error, non-compliance and missed or bad outcomes.
- We don't address avoidable demand and service failure, or we don't do so well enough, even though budgets are often under pressure.
- It's unclear how to track the rationale or progress of delivery work or operational improvement, or to know if it will achieve outcomes, despite extensive governance processes.
- It's not clear if all the investment we're making is being directed towards solving the most significant problems or opportunities.
- We miss opportunities for obvious or low-cost fixes.
- It's difficult to connect what we're working to deliver and what we want to happen, as set out by our strategy.

These aren't just any old problems. They happen because of scale, and it is valuable to solve them. Each of the chapters in this book is about them. The whole-service perspective connects what we do and change internally with the resulting performance on the outside. Redefining organizations as services to users is a profound and ambitious change, but it's also a practical approach that addresses many large-organization challenges.

There will be other problems in your organization that are not listed here. Test with people to reflect which ones are the most important or valuable to solve. Find out what's already happening in an attempt to address them. You can also check that you're on the right path by saying something like

In my experience, these are some of the key issues. Are these the most concerning ones, or are they not such a big deal from your perspective? What are you dealing with in your area? What's getting in the way?

Do the best job at solving the problems

An organization's services describe what it does in a way that matches how users would think of it. Anchoring the work we do to overall service performance gives it direction that's grounded in reality.

There are three parts to this.

1. *Measurement and evaluation of services* that takes into account users, operations and organizational outcomes. This tells us where the problems are, what's needed and what good looks like, and it gives us the case for investment.

2. *Designing and improving services* by setting up projects and improvement work with the conditions for success. This gives us the means to shape and direct work so it delivers significant value, including organizing principles and parameters to set priorities.

3. *Managing, directing and leading services* to bring clarity of vision across the organization and work as a whole team to better deliver whole services. This is about service strategy, the type of teams needed, how to coordinate work, leadership activities, planning and supportive governance.

1. How we measure and evaluate services

Mention what the 'job' of one of the main services is. Point out that people in the organization don't know if services are good or bad, what they cost or how well the supporting capabilities contribute to their performance. Relate this to the challenges you set out earlier. The performance of a service in its entirety shows us where to improve it and what is needed.

To persuade people to change how things work today, it has to feel worth it to them. Show an example of whole-service performance, a service demand funnel (see the examples in chapter 3) or an outcomes framework (see chapter 10). The example needs to reflect users, operational effort and outcomes, together. Ask how certain we are that the work we're doing today is on the right path to improve performance cohesively like this. Point out that this gives the basis to shape individual pieces of work that affect services, to keep things on track, or to see where to intervene.

A shared language helps people work together effectively. Share the work you've already done to define services and what they're made of. Ask for recommendations of other people to work with you on this.

2. How we design and improve services at scale

Identify a few of the well-known problems in one main service as a tangible example: the causes of service failure and avoidable demand, say, or the inflexibility to change because of data or technology arrangements.

Ask how much of the current work in progress is tackling these important issues? If you asked one of the teams involved, would they know what the desired results are? Work can likely be better targeted to solve known problems within or between services.

Similar types of service will have predictable problems and will potentially need similar capabilities to support them. Seeing common patterns like this in the context of services is a practical way to help teams focus on users, operations and outcomes. In the right circumstances it means that teams can address duplication and disjointed effort while reducing the risk of building or implementing 'solutions' in the abstract that don't do what's needed.

Rather than treat projects, portfolios or programmes as separate, we can see where they should be joined up by looking at them across services, or vertically through common steps in services. This helps to keep the focus on overall performance improvement, not just isolated change.

Keep it real
Don't stay abstract for too long. Include concrete examples about your own organization as you go. Talk about the things that you or other people have actually done in your organization and in organizations like yours: for example, how teams are now using a common language for service views to keep them consistent, which makes it easier to visualize and to coordinate or join up work; or how the potential financial impact of efficiency improvements has been calculated by rewriting and testing service content to better answer the questions that users have.

3. How we manage, direct and lead work

Services need coordination and leadership. They need people who can hold the vision end to end and that know how to operationalize changes, and they need operations, delivery and strategy/policy working in collaboration.

Rather than wait for a burning platform or a contract reprocurement to trigger the need for change and investment, whole-service performance becomes the basis to drive efficiency and effectiveness across services. It makes the strategic case for investment much clearer, as well as the cost–benefit analysis. As Jeff Gothelf and Josh Seiden point out in their book *Sense and Respond*, moving towards a continuous-improvement model means a 'rethinking of the way we organise and manage work'.[2]

Many industries and governments emphasize whole services now. This includes the banking, telecoms and insurance sectors, as well as central and local government. For the UK government, making services better from end to end is currently at the heart of the digital strategy.[3]

Who else has seen this?

People will want to know who else in the organization is supportive. Include a list of who you've spoken to as you go. Ask them who else you should talk to about this, and what else you should ask for that will help embed this more widely.

What needs to change: next steps

Creating true service organizations requires fundamental changes to leadership culture, strategy, governance, planning, teams and working practices. But this is too vague to get the support you need to make it happen. To start with, set out more specific changes that are relevant to your organization.

Establish a good approach for one service and iterate it
A good step forward would be to establish what good looks like for one important service. And as a collective, begin to direct and coordinate work across it so that everyone involved starts to live and breathe it. This could be a newly developing service or an existing service that's changing. It will need the support of top leadership and the right people involved day to day.

Because it's not always clear to people how profound this shift in the way of working is, you can add weight by setting out principles or beliefs that are clearly different to the default approach of the organization. And use these to embed ways of working that help teams learn what works, in reality, more quickly. For example: 'start small and iterate often', 'own the pace of delivery', 'it's about what to learn, not what to ship'. If written well and developed collaboratively, they can buy the permission to work in modern ways.

Developing good practice in one area won't necessarily have an impact on all the other areas; it takes significant changes to investment and ways of working across the entire organization.

Investment needs to go towards better services
To apply this good practice more widely, stipulate that from now on investment can only be made, or continue to be made, when there's a clear outcome that's (usually) in the context of a service or part of one. This means having a clear indication of what good looks like, along with ways of working that support continuous improvement.

This has implications for budget holders, teams that prepare business cases, and others involved in agreeing spend. We need to avoid projects that deliver 'technology' and then stop, without the desired results or with the creation of further problems.

Creating the conditions for better services requires alignment of work through changes to project framing, progress reporting and governance.

Services teams and leaders should proactively identify opportunities and initiate new work to improve them, negotiating priorities with managers of supporting capabilities.

Modern ways of working to create better service organizations
Our goal is to embed changes across the organization to make improving services the default practice. People will ask: 'How is this different to what happens currently?' It could mean:

- The various areas that have an impact on how well services work start to develop stronger service improvement approaches and capabilities. This could include hiring and training specialists in services, agreeing a list of services, changing how they work or what they work on to improve service performance and working together much more closely. These areas could include digital, data and technology, change management, organization design, strategy and policy, performance and operations, as well as centralized enabling and corporate teams.

- Organizing people and teams around important services, rather than operating from functions in isolation. Orientating the work around services, and coordinating and directing it towards improving service stages, outcomes and established performance indicators.
- An intentional shift in working practices and delivery approaches to move decision making much closer to reality and to base it on evidence. For example, by testing and learning about the legitimate options before any commitments to scale supporting capabilities.
- Expectations with sponsors, leaders and other disciplines are set or reset, and it becomes clear how to lead this sort of work, without encouraging unhelpful practices or unwittingly preventing teams from doing good work.
- Strengthened support from the centre, which can include establishing service leadership and teams, communicating what good looks like, protecting the progress of teams, and developing guidance and standards and helping teams meet them. The need for this support ideally reduces over time, as the organization and its service teams develop better ways of working themselves.

Ask for endorsement, support, introductions and invitations

While setting the ambition, also ask for practical support that the person you're talking to is in a position to offer there and then. Which support is most helpful to you will depend on the organization, but here are a few examples that I and others have used in the past.

- Their support for your suggested approach in principle. This could be spoken or in writing, via recommendations or introductions. One leader set out ways of working for a programme in a blog post and gained agreement from the minister for this – which then gave them something official to refer everyone else to.

- Agreement to embed this approach as part of any operating model work, strategy or budget requests. This could include introductions to people already involved in this work, or an instruction to them to embed this.
- Introductions and invitations to speak about this at important forums, with a personal recommendation or introduction from them. This includes leadership meetings, away days, governance forums, communities of practice, and the forums of other teams.
- Specific quotes you can use with others that demonstrate their support. You can draft them up front for them to edit.
- Agreement that they will actively advocate this approach with senior leadership across the organization.
- Ask them which executive, board member or other senior leader would be the right person to represent and lead this (even if unofficial or hypothetical, for now).
- Ask them to agree to broker your involvement in spend and budgeting processes and ask them to help champion the focus on outward-facing service performance as the means to drive internal improvement.
- A commitment that they will bring their influence to bear in encouraging, supporting or mandating that teams will work in these ways, wherever it is valuable to do so.
- Ask them to mention this work in their communications, such as blog posts, week notes and internal memos, or in conversation as they circulate within the organization (you can help by giving them a paragraph to work with).
- Ask for their suggestions for key individuals to form a group of people steering this, to make sure it's genuinely cross-functional and multidisciplinary and represents important interests.

- To support by helping to remove blockers to service improvement work: for example, request greater autonomy within service teams to improve service content, outside the corporate comms teams.
- Recommendations for who else you should talk to about this, and who you should work with.
- Ask for follow-up meetings with them so that they continue to support and help you to remove blockers, i.e. sponsorship.
- The time and space for an enabling team to support areas of the organization to make this real: for example, by defining services organization-wide, mapping the main services, or establishing performance indicators.

Find your audience

Start testing these messages, even before you know who the right people are. Begin by showing someone. That person will suggest someone else, and so on. The more iterations you do, the better and more actionable this narrative will become. Then figure out who the right people are. These will be leadership and other influencers across the organization: the people who could have an amplifying effect to embed this thinking across the entire organization.

You can't go in cold or in the wrong order. Wait until you've got a concise story that works before talking to the most influential people. You might need to develop a relationship first, or at least be introduced by someone else. Get it wrong and you can be seen as wasting people's time, thereby losing the initiative. Get advice from those who are experienced with navigating the organization. Ask what it would take to embed this approach in your particular organization – who to test it with, who to talk to, and in what order. You don't need lots of people. And you don't need them all at once. This can take place over time. Test it. Iterate.

Position yourself to benefit from coming across valuable people. You could mention it as some work that folks may want to be made aware of. That's an easy ask because it doesn't require any input on their part. You'll quickly hear about connections with other pieces of work or people doing something they think might overlap.

Services are not the only story

It's important to realize that your work or approach won't be the only thing being developed. What you're working on or talking to people about could be inconsistent or in conflict with other work happening at the same time. You can get yourself an invitation to a conversation or an important introduction by saying you would appreciate a steer for how to link this work or strengthen it by aligning it with an existing or emerging strategy. People appreciate attempts to avoid unnecessary confusion and overlap in a large organization. Even if what you're creating couldn't be more different, it can be a relief to others that you're at least keen to be aware of all the related work.

Prepare a five-minute version

Meetings get cut short. This doesn't mean your message isn't important. It happens to everyone, including the chief executive. When it happens to you, having a short version will mean you don't waste time scrambling through it.

Get the whole story down to three main points and four or five slides. This is a good exercise because it forces you to be very clear and concise, which is helpful to everyone. The simpler you can make your story, the more likely others will take it on and tell people about it.

Share this short version ahead of in-person meetings to give people the chance to gather their thoughts. Most don't have time to read ahead, but when you reach someone who does, it means you can use the time together to discuss next steps instead.

Join forces with other leaders and influencers

Find the people who have similar concerns to you and can help: the influential leaders with the power or the budget who, if they were driving this themselves, would make it go a lot faster – and with whose support your job would be easier. This is likely to include the CEO, the COO, the CIO and the CFO; the chief of digital, data and technology; the chief executive, director general, permanent secretary or managing director; as well as other executives and members of the board whose job it is to set strategy. In the public sector it could include politicians. If it's not obvious, try directors or people involved in change, digital, transformation, innovation, operations or improvement work. Ask them who else you should speak to.

Get to know the interests and concerns of individuals. If you're working without support from the top, you'll need good relationships with a great many more people at the level below the top to help make up for it. Even in these top positions, you – and they – still need to be convincing to many others to win support.

It's difficult to get in with this group if you're starting from scratch. But it's not where you start – it's where you work towards once you've got valuable things to say and something tangible to present. Fortunately, in large organizations there are plenty of other well-positioned and influential people to get to know. They can be in almost any role. They've likely been there a long time. They'll be well regarded across the organization. They usually have the ear of others who are influential and powerful. Through networks like these you can reach all the people you need. And you don't always have to rely on top-down cover if you have the right support across the organization anyway. As one chief of staff said to me, 'You don't need [top person's] support. It's not political, it's common sense. You can still do all that you need to without them.'

To identify the right people in your organization, consider the following questions.

- Who has budget and who influences spend?
- Who sets strategy?
- Who works closely with those who influence spend or set strategy, but who may be more available to you?
- Who is currently initiating projects in ways that are contrary to this approach? Who else is already concerned about the shape of work (even if for different reasons)?
- Who tracks current portfolios and work that impacts services?
- Whose priorities and issues are related to the same underlying conditions that a greater focus on services would help address?
- Who struggles with underfunded and overworked operations and is already concerned with avoidable demand that this approach might help win support for?
- Who else has similar goals in mind, even if their practices are incredibly different? The CFO and the finance team will be interested in efficiency. Economists will have an interest in performance analysis. Architects (the enterprise, business or technical kind) are interested in coordinating, strengthening and rationalizing supporting capability and activity, as well as reducing duplication.

Pair up with people who can navigate the organization and leadership

If you aren't sure how to navigate your organization and its various levels of bureaucracy, you haven't the time to learn, and if this is all new territory to you, it can be incredibly valuable to pair up with someone else who is already good at this. Many people are already adept at working up and down a large organization. Most organizations will have many others who understand institutional bureaucracy and are interested in using their experience to bring about productive change. They may benefit from developing a better understanding of your world and experience in return. They can put you in a stronger position in meetings with the right people. And, in turn, you can help them gain experience in other fields.

Anticipate challenge and design for it

Prepare for some inevitable and appropriate challenge by anticipating the ways in which someone could completely disagree with the principle of focusing on services and their performance. Write them down. Focus on the questions that are hard or uncomfortable – because these will be the genuinely good challenges.

No single proposed model or approach has all the answers for every situation. Every context is different. We're putting this thinking to work, making it genuinely valuable in a real context – not delivering some abstract ideal. It's not about pretending this is perfect or that it applies universally in every context. But the ideas in this book are good ways to address many important issues that are very common in large service-providing organizations.

Here are some good challenges to start with, some of which you may recognize from experience.

- Let's fix the basics first shall we? We don't need the gold standard, just good enough. We need to 'keep the lights on'.
- I agree with this, but you haven't got a chance of landing it here.
- My main problem or priority is one that doesn't appear to be addressed by what you are suggesting.
- We've got so much going on. This sounds like yet another thing we have to do on top of all the other things. It sounds like a lot. I don't think we have the time, funding, capacity or resources available for this.

- I agree with it, but I'm unable to – or I'm not going to – do anything to support it. It's down to you to do this, if you think you have the time.
- We're already doing this. It's not clear how this is different to the enterprise architecture strategy, the product strategy, the customer experience strategy, our portfolio strategy, or any other strategy that we have agreed on and are pursuing.
- What you're talking about is exactly what we're doing. We're refreshing the core IT systems and fixing the data that underpin most of what you're talking about, so that should give a big improvement.
- We can't even look at our services until we've fixed all the technology and data first, and that will take five years.
- Services are the wrong thing to focus on. We need to think about change at a systemic level. There's too much wrong thinking and duplication that won't be solved unless we address it at the highest level possible.
- Why are you talking about services in particular? Why don't we just apply what you're saying to our tech refresh programmes or to our policymaking and strategy?
- Why services? Why don't you advocate focusing on humans, society, the environment or the climate?
- This all sounds very much like upfront design and not at all agile. It will slow things down.
- This is good, but what we really need to focus on are corporate services and internal tools for staff. Staff are users too. We need to look at our HR systems, our finance systems and the big intranet project. We're procuring a new enterprise resource planning tool – that's where this thinking could bring real value.

Work with a few people to develop responses that work. Build these responses into what you say as you run through the narrative with people. This helps people appreciate that you do get where they're coming from and that you understand their fears. Make a note of any good new challenges that come your way.

- 'You're probably wondering why I'm talking about services rather than the projects we have in progress?'
- 'At this point you might be thinking, doesn't this add to the problem of duplicating technology?'
- 'Some people think this will take longer, but really it brings forward what was going to derail us anyway.'
- 'You might be thinking this will need funding when we're already trying to reduce spending. But it's really about cost saving by removing wasted effort and service failure.'

Summary

① Tell the story in a way that sets out how thinking in terms of whole services and outcomes helps address important organization issues.

② Cover how to measure and evaluate services; how to design and improve them at scale; and what this means for managing, directing and leading the work. Finish by setting out what needs to change specifically and asking for practical support.

③ Test the narrative and iterate it until you get to something that makes sense to most people.

④ Create a version that you could run through in less than five minutes and that someone could quickly skim through before a meeting to get the main points.

⑤ Find the people in the organization who can tell you how to bring about profound change 'around here': who to talk to, what their priorities are, how to get a meeting with them, what's important, what are the influential forums and groups to engage with.

⑥ Do this well and many different professions should be able to see that it reflects their interests too, whether that's people, strategy, policy, operations, data or technology. It's a practical approach that isn't at odds with the focus of other disciplines.

Chapter 13

Make better services the organization's strategy

Don't forget about the significant cost of maintaining the status quo option or approach. This is often presented as if it's a neutral 'do nothing' option that 'avoids investment' or risk, but it can be very far from that.[1]

Driving the performance of services across your entire organization can't just rely on you. It needs to be an integral part of how organizations operate by default. Many of the chapters in this book have been about embedding services at the heart of how the organization operates. This chapter offers additional steps to increase the momentum and scale of this profound change.

There will be other mechanisms and activities that are relevant to your organization or industry, but let's look at five ways to put the focus on services and their performance.

Embed whole services in organizational strategy, planning and budgets

Creating the conditions for better-performing, joined-up services *is* an organizational strategy. It's a way of seeing the organization in a new light and of operating and prioritizing that has widespread implications. It's not about doing good service design in just a few places.

It's not just a 'nice idea' to orchestrate organizations around services to users either: it is central to their success. The whole point is to improve effectiveness and efficiency, with the added benefit of coordinating operations, capabilities, design, change and investment.

To embed it at a deeper level, make this narrative part of existing or emerging organizational strategy. This includes all the missions, plans or visions that all large organizations construct from time to time. Whatever the purpose, aim to include content about making services more coherent and better performing across the whole. If better services are part of the official strategy, this will help increase the credibility and legitimacy of your work.

Influential individuals will be able to guide you to the planning activity and events where strategy and funding are determined. If you can embed the idea of using whole-service performance to shape and improve delivery and operational work, it can help to set the wheels in motion for the years to come.

You'll need to understand enough of the political context and priorities to make it unarguable why creating better services is relevant and important right now: for example, financial constraints and budget cuts; environment and climate goals; inequity across a region or population; concerns about exposure to debt or fraud; lack of visibility of data to understand and manage financial risk; and failures in service provision to the right people. Making better services touches on so many of the problems large organizations grapple with that it's not hard to place the emphasis on the current priority. Those who understand the institution can provide the background. This doesn't make all the other reasons to create better services any less valid, but it does give you a more urgent and compelling story for the context you work within.

Involve yourself in planning work that's often happening somewhere in the organization. You get the added benefit of hearing or reading about what else is happening and what people are thinking about. The authors are often relieved when someone offers draft text for consideration in important areas. At the very least, offer to read drafts to help people avoid conflicting or inaccurate messages about services, users, digital or technology before it goes to senior leaders.

Make bold recommendations: things like taking a test-and-learn approach to reduce risk, connecting proposed work with known problems to solve, or improving services based on real-world performance. Add a reference to a list of services to make it tangible. Mention specific priorities for service improvement work, as well as a general approach to join up individual pieces of work and help protect investment. Doing this creates less risky delivery approaches across portfolios. If you can bring to bear clear thinking, logic and rationale, it can end up being reflected back in concrete plans for investment.

Crises, audits and other major events also provide the grounds for steering the organization into creating the conditions to help everyone else create better services.

Follow the money

Get to know what the money circulating within the organization is for, where it's going and why, and how the investment process works. Knowing how the money flows (and where it sits currently) puts you in a better position to direct it towards more valuable outcomes, or to draw on your experience and skills to reduce the risk.

But how do we obtain funding for better services and more continuous improvement? And what can we do if it isn't working well at the moment? Traditional funding models weren't designed for teams that design and deliver continuously, while learning and then iterating what they do. A 2021 report 'Fixing

Digital Funding in Government' describes the issues and sets out recommendations for how to change funding to better support digital ways of working (many of which apply to large companies too).[2] But there are a few ways to operate within and around some of the current constraints.[3]

How to obtain funding
In a large service-providing organization, it's likely that much of the existing investment in work that is underway *is* part of or *will* affect services – it's just not shaped in a way that recognizes this, or it is not directed towards improving service performance. At worst, funding is tied up in risky, large, predetermined endeavours that don't allow for learning and iteration. Teams might be hiring people without realizing there are modern professions that specialize in exactly the problems they need to be tackling.

Existing investment will always be the more significant 'pot'. Get to know the work in detail, particularly the underlying goals or desired outcomes. Talk to people who share concerns about its success or contribution. Prepare a short list of the validated issues, together with ideas about reducing risk and uncertainty: by embedding an approach that gathers evidence to determine the right (or more right) direction, for example.

Smaller and more frequent cycles of funding are one way to encourage evidence gathering for service improvement and to reduce the financial risk of large-programme failure.[4] This can be aligned with a managed life cycle for investment (see chapter 11) or a spend control process.[5] This isn't an easy change to make, and it needs a group of influential people working together with the finance team to plan for this.

Another more immediate way is to find sources of smaller amounts of money. Just enough funding to seed ideas: small amounts of work to prove or disprove that it could be well worth investing further. This could come from 'innovation pots' or from philanthropic sources. Budget is often repurposed or resequenced from existing large programmes or from existing budget holders. Find ways for your organization to fund small ideas to evidence and grow.

Find the people who know when budgets are drafted, reviewed and changed, and get involved. This might not help in the short term but it could secure what's needed down the line.

Ask for copies of successful business cases and write more of them yourselves. These don't always need to be formal documents, at least not straight away. Depending on where you work, it could start with an email, a short paper or a slide deck that sets out a compelling argument and opportunity for leadership or budget holders and planners.

Help others grow confidence and understanding about how money enters and flows across the organization, and how they themselves can support or create compelling cases for investment and change. This should become an integral part of many professional career and learning pathways.[6]

What to do about the 'wrong sort of budget'
It's common in large organizations for a significant proportion of budget to be earmarked for one-off investments, known as capital expenditure. This type of spend doesn't reflect modern operations and ways of working: that is, the people and teams required to develop, manage, improve and iterate important capabilities including technology on an ongoing basis. This isn't just 'desirable', the reality is that in the digital era it can be dangerous not to continually develop technology capabilities once they exist. Supporting people to do this requires ongoing funding that is classed as 'operational' or 'resource' expenditure, which many organizations (or rather, traditional funding models) try to limit. But to be properly managed, looked after, evaluated and improved, services need suitable operational expenditure.[7]

Without it, hiring permanent individuals and establishing teams becomes difficult, particularly for modern disciplines and capabilities that aren't yet well understood by the rest of the organization. You need support from the top to change this situation – and you should ask whether that support is available before you join a new organization.

If you're in a position to, it's a great idea to develop and maintain good working relationships with the finance director and their team, as well as everyone else involved in budgetary planning. Make sure that enough people are aware of this issue to help address it in the next budgeting cycle or financial planning event.

All that said, many organizations have been able to work within these constraints to create the conditions for ongoing service development and improvement. Some do this by developing sequential business cases to maintain the people, teams and effort that were previously funded as a one off. One major public service has successfully made twenty-two different business cases that have helped it to evolve and grow over the years in the absence of ongoing funding. This requires effort and it can be frustrating, but having the wrong kind of budget doesn't always prevent what's needed. And a one-off investment or time-limited programme can at least shine a light on what's genuinely worth investing in on a continuous basis.

Make the case for better service funding
The ideas in chapter 3 help to identify what are likely to be some of the biggest opportunities in terms of strategic value as well as cost–benefit. If teams are doing exploratory discovery work or are aiming to establish modern working practice, steer them towards making this a more compelling case for investment by understanding what will bring significant *value* for the context.

Part of this is making the argument about the significant cost of maintaining the status quo approach, and the missed opportunities and increased risk involved.

Make the case for ongoing funding of permanent teams and outcomes, with ways of working that mean the work can be (re)prioritized as needed. As examples in chapter 7 showed, it's more efficient to establish – and then to protect – a few core teams that are used to working together than it is to have to stand up a new team from scratch each time.

Identify what else 'drives' the changes you're recommending.[8] It might be to do with efficiency or effectiveness, or it could be to do with changing culture or reducing risk. Being clear yourself – and helping everyone else be clear – about what difference that makes to the health of the organization makes it a much easier step to create a business case for. Whether that's reducing the unit cost of being able to make changes, reducing the cycle time of learning and delivery, or reducing the number of people involved per deal closed.

*

This is just a very brief introduction to working with, and within, budgets to embed whole-service approaches. We're all learning how to do this better.

Structure the organization around services

Much of this book could be viewed as organization design for service organizations, but the advice in it hasn't relied on making radical changes to structure. So far I've talked about teams, functions and leadership working together over the top of some of the current structures to cross boundaries and connect disparate activities. This puts creating the conditions for a much stronger focus on services within reach of most organizations.

But there are more profound changes to aim for. To break from Conway's law,[9] orient organizations around their users, services and outcomes rather than around their existing internal structures. This shift helps to turn older organizations and institutions into true service organizations.

Doing this will include reorganizing parts of the organization to support end-to-end services, making whole-service performance the guiding beacon. Instead of separate functions such

Figure 12. Structuring teams around services.

as strategy, operations, delivery and policy working to their own plans, form multidisciplinary teams to work on or across services, wherever it makes sense to. Move towards leadership and ongoing improvement of whole services, underpinned by supporting capabilities and enabling teams.

This represents a big change to the shape of many of our institutions, but it isn't just theory and it's not a new idea.[10] Many large organizations and significant change programmes are already doing this in both the private and public sectors.[11] This includes banks, telecoms, insurers and parts of government (I include examples at the end of this chapter). Some have been set up radically differently from the start. Others are making incremental changes towards structuring around services.

Position teams and individuals to shape, govern and join up work

Seek out the people who have already seen the need to orchestrate the organization around its users and services and are attempting to move in that direction. They could be from any background: operations, policy, technology, user-centred design, product, architecture. Help to place these individuals in a position to influence important processes, or work with them to do so, to have an amplifying effect on the whole organization.

This can include

- processes through which work is governed, assessed and steered;
- shaping and setting up new work and investment, especially where delivery approaches are being established;
- development of policy or strategic options where strategy and high-level direction will be explored up front;
- coordinating and joining up teams for whole service improvement (this could include connecting teams working to improve individual parts of services, re-establishing feedback loops between the work and real-world performance, helping everyone understand whole-service measurement and success, or using views of whole services to identify the work needed to fill gaps or connect activity); and
- placing these people in roles and in forums of influence, including senior leadership teams, executive teams, committees, authorities and boards, especially where these are currently populated by people who represent only some of the important functions, backgrounds or specialist skills.

Hire whole-service specialists
There are specialist professions that have a greater proportion of individuals with the skills and knowledge to do aspects of this well. These include service designers, user researchers, content designers, product managers and service owners. These disciplines are vital in delivery teams working to change and improve services, but they also have a huge impact when they are able to work between and across individual teams. This could be through

- identifying and sharing good practice and standards more widely;
- rethinking how something could work radically better;
- improving and joining up a whole service to work better within or across organizations;
- reshaping individual projects to make them more likely to improve service performance; or
- pairing up with parts of the organization to help direct where investment is made, how new initiatives are established, or how governance works, to better orchestrate the organization around its services.

One way to sow the seeds for this is to centrally fund these specialists, initially in new roles, to place them in the right parts of the organization 'for free'. Organizations such as DEFRA have funded such roles for an initial six-month period. This gives organizations some flexibility to embed people strategically. By doing this, the team – or the area or process they work with – gets extra help, while everyone gets to learn what's most valuable for a particular context. It's a stronger basis to then negotiate and agree how to make roles and capabilities like these sustainable, as well as agreeing on the conditions needed for the activity to be worthwhile.

Other organizations have added these newer specialist roles to central governance and decision-making forums. These are the places where new work is given shape, or where work in progress is steered, in situations outside service teams and leadership. They work with colleagues to add the often-missing focus on the impact or opportunity for customer-facing parts of services, making this one of the primary considerations where needed.

Position specialists at these points across the organization. They can have a greater impact collectively on the performance of services across the organization than they do if they are kept within just one team.

Training and coaching for board members, executives and leaders

Hearing from afar about the benefits of structuring around services is very different to living and breathing this change as a leader. How to drive and support the changes needed to be a true service organization won't be obvious to all. Some will instinctively do what's needed, others will be curious. Some will be resistant, while others will think they're already doing what's needed.

One way to make the required changes clear is to provide practical training on service leadership. But it needs to cover what's involved at different levels.

Provide training on whole-service leadership
This might include how genuinely multidisciplinary teams operate and what it means as a leader to support them to work across a service. It also means how to hold this bigger picture while being involved in day-to-day decision making and prioritization, tackling the hard trade-offs. It's been important for other leaders to learn how to create the right conditions around the service: reorganizing the governance; putting processes in place to coordinate, support and empower teams; bringing operations, policy and digital delivery together; setting a clear service strategy and supportive communications.

Managing a programme or portfolio of work that affects services
Working at this level means being able to lead effectively when the work influences or impacts many different services, while at the same time structuring teams and work to productively develop, iterate and scale the supporting tools, products, platforms and other capabilities.

How leaders can create the wider conditions needed
There are many leadership activities needed to make better services a core part of the organization's agenda, and to grow the

awareness, capabilities and processes so that everyone else is able to lead and deliver successful services on an ongoing basis. Supporting leaders to develop the skills and experience could form part of a career path or be provided as continuing professional development.

*

Some organizations carry out leadership training before a major service goes live, or ahead of a significant programme of modernization that affects a service. It helps leaders to see what the organization is trying to do in a different way and what's really involved in managing a continuously running and improving service, and it helps equip them for this. Different things will be needed from them as service leaders. How they work and how teams and processes are set up for a service to improve on an ongoing basis can be completely different to what they've experienced in other parts of the organization.

It's not just service leaders that need this service leadership training: it's the entire executive team and the directors. Executives won't necessarily understand the implications and the real benefits of working in this way – of setting up services differently for iterative change and improvement.

All of this involves leadership moving much closer to the reality of operations and the people that use services. This includes observing people trying to use the service, and those who support it, or undertaking training using a test environment, and participating in role plays with realistic scenarios in which leaders used to operating at a distance are faced with what really happens.

Help boards challenge others in the right way
Board members scrutinize and challenge organizations, their leadership and their strategy. This means they're well placed to steer a path towards better approaches to services.

Running awareness sessions, training and coaching for boards, executives and leadership teams helps bring constructive challenge and influence back to an organization. Others in scrutinizing roles and teams can benefit too: the finance, regulatory and audit teams, for example. It's increasingly well understood that boards need awareness of digital transformation and modern technology practices from reliable sources. Knowing how to orchestrate pieces of work, people, capabilities and processes in a way that results in better services across the whole helps put this in context for service organizations.

It's worth getting to know an individual on the board, or finding the people inside the organization who already have that relationship and work through them. This is not so you can bombard them with all the usual problems inherent in any large organization but so that you can listen to their concerns and make them aware of the two or three valuable opportunities they can consider raising, in addition to their own challenges.

*

With all that set, you should be in a much stronger position to have an outsized effect on the service organization you work with.

It's time for a final review of everything we've covered.

Summary

① Make the narrative about better-performing services an integral part of organizational strategy and investment cases.

② Many organizations are now structuring their entire operation around whole services, reducing the separation between functions, supported by service leadership, coordinating and cross-cutting teams.

③ Join forces with other individuals who work to connect and integrate functions across the organization.

④ Hire service specialists and position them to best influence how important processes work across the organization.

⑤ Demonstrate whole-service ways of working to leaders and influential individuals across the organization.

⑥ Equip leaders, boards and executives with the means to bring influence, scrutiny and challenge to help create the conditions for better services through training and awareness sessions.

Orientating a global organization around customer goals
BT Group plc
It's been said that large organizations have just two speeds for major change: extremely slow and overnight.

BT Group plc is one of the world's leading communications services companies, operating the BT, EE and Plusnet brands.

I spoke to Conor Ward, director of design in BT's Consumer Digital team, who described to me the profound changes BT have made to focus on what's important to their customers and users:[12]

> BT established a new incarnation of its Consumer (business to customer facing) Digital & Design teams in 2018. But the radical approach they took to do this – together with senior leadership support – has had a big impact on the organization.
>
> Many organizations will choose to start with one agile user-centred product squad, focusing on an exemplar project that serves as a 'lighthouse' to showcase modern ways of working, deliver value early, and then scale from there. Instead, BT's Digital Consumer unit took a very different approach and decided to land this new digital-first, product-focused, agile and user-centred operating model across its digital products all at once.

BT put in place a 'three-legged-stool' leadership team of new digital directors representing product, design and engineering in equal partnership alongside an agile capability director. Together they very quickly established 100 new multidisciplinary product squads and transferred all work from existing siloed functions and projects, in a matter of weeks.

The newly formed squads were restructured into clusters called 'tribes' and were loosely organized around groups of customer goals that had close links to existing business activity, to senior leaders and to the underlying technology estate. In the Design space, new roles were established such as product design, content design, service design, user research, accessibility and design operations, by hiring specialists. At the same time, existing staff were upskilled through training and coaching programmes to achieve scale and to rapidly grow maturity.

Service designers facilitated activities across the tribes to help them to agree on common terms such as 'service', 'journey' and 'user goal'. This shared lexicon helped to improve communication about what the squads were working on and how all the work related.

Service designers also helped the tribes to draw on existing research to define the things that BT customers are fundamentally trying to get done. This was critical to help us understand how to organize ourselves efficiently. One important principle was to only allow silos where the effect least matters, or is least apparent, to customers. These customer goals and journeys were published in a central 'journey framework'. And a working group was created to support the advocacy and governance of the framework. This framework has also helped us improve how we are measuring experience consistently across journeys.

In 2021 BT Group then brought in a chief digital and innovation officer, who created a new combined digital function across the entire BT Group which took control of all digital change and delivery work centrally, tasked with accelerating the Group. This had two profound effects. Firstly, they were able to roll out the idea of organizing and structuring around customer goals, services and outcomes more widely, and set clear performance indicators, across the organization. Secondly, they could then prioritize significant improvements needed across the whole estate: developing and improving supporting capabilities, removing legacy technology, and transforming all the external customer-facing touchpoints – it's difficult for individual business units alone to identify, prioritize or align on significant transformation that cuts across their areas. These changes have embedded a focus on users, outcomes and the transformation of end-to-end services.

Conor added:

Changing the organization on this scale, this quickly, has been very exciting but also very challenging. We continue to iterate how we operate, and that can sometimes feel like constant change from all angles. But it's how we leapfrogged away from traditional, waterfall processes to more modern, user-centred services, capabilities and ways of working in a matter of months, rather than years.

We also needed to change the approach to design. When it started, we focused on creating a design strategy, assessing our user-centred design maturity, and 'how we're going to help the organization become more user centred'. It became clear quite quickly that this approach was all a bit too insular and siloed in our thinking. Because of how we've now organized and structured around our customers at our core, our approach as a design function has become: 'What are we all trying to achieve together as a business for our customers and how can we help?'

It's less about evangelizing design, and more about getting on with being helpful, aligning to a genuinely shared strategy and vision, with a holistic cross functional team truly focused on customer needs. Our design strategy is now merely another method of contributing to product strategy, and company strategy, which has helped ensure success.

Structuring the organization as a service
HM Passport Office, UK
HM Passport Office is the issuer of UK passports and is responsible for civil registration services in England & Wales through the General Register Office.

Colin Foley, head of business and service design, explains how viewing the organization in terms of the end-to-end passport service and improving whole-service performance became the foundation of redesigning parts of the organization.[13]

> We began to view the organization in a different way: around the end-to-end service, rather than the functional silos, organizing and structuring ourselves to help with problematic decision processes, as well as processes that underpin the organization.
>
> Users sit at the top, and you build the case by showing how and where it doesn't work well and what the impact of that is. Even with the best of intentions, the flow of decisions wasn't as efficient as it could be, and that caused problems for the service. We needed to bring people together across functions, to try to fix these problems; for the customer, but also for efficiency of operations.
>
> The end-to-end service became a concept for organization redesign. You need something that allows you to manage and view the business as a full service; that helps you drive decisions to improve its performance overall. There's lots of activity in individual parts or in geographical regions, but the functional silos we had aren't just about individual tasks. We deliver this service universally, which involves casework, customer contact, technology, logistics. If you're going to organize as a service, you have to think about what work is best done by thinking across the whole (and then iterating, tailoring it and customizing as needed), what work is best done by enabling and facilitating services, and how do you then measure and manage it all.
>
> We knew that decision making around the service needed to improve: how we use insight about customers, or about fraud;

how to guide decisions made by suppliers, and what data would allow us to do that. Rather than it being an abstract concept removed from the reality of operations, we could map this all to decision making around the actual service and individual stages. It gave us the basis for consensus about how to 'steer the car' – by focusing activity on the service and the end goal for the customer.

We evolved the organization by working together. We all wanted this to work well, we had shared motivations about the service we're trying to deliver and improve. What helped was focusing on the activities needed for it to work well, rather than looking directly at the org structure. We set out the activities we do, how they are organized, what work we have to do to deliver the whole service, and how we'd know if we were doing it well. Because we were talking about the activities rather than the teams, it was easier to move to consensus: what to change, what to keep, how it is run and the overarching management of it.

Making continuous improvement a precondition for funding
The Home Office, UK

Financing and accounting practices in large organizations can work against modern digital delivery approaches. The split between capital and operational expenditure suits upfront policymaking and legislating, if the plan is to outsource predetermined work that results in assets. But it doesn't work for teams to iteratively develop and continuously improve capabilities to support better end-to-end services.[14]

In practice, this can mean having to establish a 'change programme' to try to deliver significant improvement or new capability (using capital expenditure) rather than making change and improvement an integral part of 'business as usual' (BAU) teams who run and maintain services (using operational expenditure) – because of constraints in how funding works. Yet the goal is to have people that run services working together with people who deliver the improvement work, mutually learning what works best – not separating those that 'change' from those that 'run'.

Another problem is when change programmes reach the end of their planned period, often without available funding for continuous improvement. Organizations are faced with operating and missed-opportunity costs that haven't been anticipated or accounted for, creating a cycle of 'boom and bust'.

In government, this negates the view that departments and organizations can themselves be 'value creators' by building internal teams and the necessary capability to deliver, improve and iterate better services, more efficiently.

The Home Office is the UK government department responsible for immigration, security, law and order. Rob Thompson is the chief technology officer and Katy Arnold is the former deputy director for experience and strategy delivery within the Digital, Data and Technology directorate. Together they've been working with leadership across the department to create the conditions to support continuous improvement of services. One example of this is by addressing funding to prevent this cycle repeating. They explain:

> We're trialling a new funding and governance model that supports continuous improvement and iteration. Rather than 'closing' some of the programmes that were due to end in this current financial cycle, which is the UK government's 'spend review' or 'SR', we've made ongoing funding available for the teams that adopt iterative ways of working to improve the products and other parts of services they've developed continuously. It means teams can focus on delivering value by continuously improving capability, without lengthy investment processes and administration each time. We now have more permanent teams continuously improving the products and tools that support important services: helping operational staff with task management at the UK border, for example.

We established these new ways of working together with portfolio leadership by making the case that the traditional model of 'change programme' versus 'BAU' isn't in line with contemporary standards for delivery of modern services that are supported by digital and technology capability. In fact, the whole organization would benefit from having a much closer relationship to the performance of services, products, technology and processes that operationalize its policies. The benefits of adopting new practices are reduced delivery risk, reduced cost of ownership and operation of services, reduced administration, and greater empowerment of staff, while making it simpler, clearer and easier for users, with a higher likelihood of meeting policy intent.

Despite the clear benefits, adopting new ways of working is a cultural challenge. The timing was important. There were deliverability risks with one portfolio which gave the opportunity and urgency to do things differently. But to make changes at this scale you also need organizational legitimacy; we brokered agreement with the department's main investment committee, which gave the cover this needed.

You need a coalition of the willing to get going, with senior air cover. You need to appeal to hearts as well as minds. Because it involves changing long-held beliefs about how to deliver, it comes with a grieving process and a period of adjustment; you have to let people go through that.

Although the UK government has spending controls and the service standard, relying on these alone doesn't influence the changes to the business and culture required for transformation in large organizations; but these are foundational to success. You have to understand what the main forces are that hold current culture in place. You don't change working practice by preaching to people or telling them they're wrong.

You've got to work with the grain, not against it, to bring about significant change. In our case that was with the flow of money across the organization. Creating the right conditions requires engagement, support, iterating and improving along the way. It's an approach to cultural and behavioural change that encourages modern working practice but gives it real effect by making it conditional to obtaining ongoing funding.

Most services transcend an individual team or function
The Department for Environment, Food & Rural Affairs, UK: service and user centred design
Lynne Roberts is the deputy director of user-centred design and Cathy Dutton is the head of interaction and service design. Together they are currently responsible for more than sixty designers and user researchers working with teams across DEFRA. Collectively, their focus is on introducing and supporting whole-service design and leadership approaches across the department.[15]
Cathy explains:

We now have service designers working across our flood, farming and trade portfolios of work, outside of individual delivery teams. They help visualize a service as the end user would know it. They connect teams and help to design the interactions and building blocks that make up services. They also give shape to new work, by establishing the problems, the costs, the issues to prioritize, and the people and skills that are likely to be needed. Service designers work with the wider organization too, including our policy teams, to understand what we already have and know, and they work together to define outcomes. These outcomes give the direction for the work that a delivery team might then be involved with.

Summary

The conditions inside organizations can be intentionally designed and refined so that everyone consistently provides better-performing services. What follows below are the foundations required to deliver and lead successful services, sustainably.

To create more outward-facing organizations, *define the services they provide to users*. Services describe what the organization does in a way that matches how users would think of it. Anchoring pieces of work to how they affect overall service performance gives direction that's grounded in reality.

Establish a common language for what services are made of, and a genuinely shared model for modernization to help people work together. Size up the opportunity to improve services. Look at performance indicators across the whole. Use this as the basis to shape and direct the work that affects services.

Set the direction for a service or group of services by *establishing an overarching strategy that's ambitious but practical*. Organizing principles and parameters will help guide the work of teams, who need outcomes to aim for that are free from implied solutions. Specific types of multidisciplinary team are needed to work across complex services.

Steer programmes and portfolios towards outcomes. Put in place assessment of work in progress that considers users, deliverability, strategy, risk and cost.

Service organizations need *leaders who can see – and are able to protect – the overall vision* on behalf of users, operations and organizational goals. They know what it means to lead change operationally, and they can corral other influences to protect priorities and deliverability. Teams need to be structured to be relatively self-organizing, but large services that are changing significantly can require coordinating, to steer and align the work of others, until a more settled working rhythm is established.

Planning needs to reflect the reality of more complex service delivery. This means plans that change or accrue more detail as we learn what's actually needed, what works and what doesn't.

Bring governance and accountability closer to the work in hand. Embed it as a life cycle of how work moves across the organization, to shape its effect on services. Shape and control how new investment is granted to protect and remove risk. The ability to intervene when things don't go so well is necessary for services and organizations at scale. Make sure that those with operational experience and those with knowledge of customers and users, and of modern ways of working, are an integral part of decision making. Put decision making and recommending responsibility with the teams closest to the work, while making coordinators, senior leaders and stakeholders readily available for major changes or impact, oversight and escalation.

Bold and ambitious change to create true service organizations needs *support from the top* to put services at the heart of how the organization operates and address the problems and opportunities that individuals most care about.

Position people and specialists in such a way that they can influence how work is seen, shaped, steered and governed to result in better services across the whole. *Embed service approaches in organizational strategy.*

Structure the organization around services, using whole-service performance as the guiding beacon, supported by capabilities and teams able to iterate to improve performance.

Further resources and reading

You can find me at katetarling.com, along with tools, resources and links to blog posts and people that might help and inspire you.

The list of people, writing and talks that informed what's in this book is huge. In many parts it is a curation of current knowledge and thinking. Here are just a few of the books that helped me to write this one.

Strategy, ideas and advice for large organizations

Azeem Azhar. 2021. *Exponential: How Accelerating Technology Is Leaving Us Behind and What to Do about It.* Random House Business.

Marianne Bellotti. 2021. *Kill It with Fire: Manage Aging Computer Systems (And Future Proof Modern Ones).* No Starch Press.

John Cutler. *The Beautiful Mess 2020.* A collection of ideas and guides available at https://johnpcutler.github.io/tbm2020/.

Jeff Gothelf and Josh Seiden. 2017. *Sense & Respond: How Successful Organizations Listen to Customers and Create New Products Continuously.* Harvard Business Press.

Andrew Greenway, Ben Terrett, Mike Bracken and Tom Loosemore. 2021. *Digital Transformation at Scale: Why the Strategy Is Delivery,* 2nd edition. London Publishing Partnership.

Chris Risdon and Patrick Quattlebaum. 2018. *Orchestrating Experiences: Collaborative Design for Complexity.* Rosenfeld Media.

Richard Rumelt. 2017. *Good Strategy, Bad Strategy: The Difference and Why It Matters.* Profile Books.

Marc Stickdorn. 2016. *This Is Service Design Doing: Applying Service Design Thinking in the Real World*. O'Reilly Media.

Shaping, organizing and structuring work and teams

Marty Cagan with Chris Jones. 2020. *Empowered: Ordinary People, Extraordinary Products*. Wiley.

Douglas W. Hubbard. 2014. *How to Measure Anything: Finding the Value of Intangibles in Business*, 3rd edition. Wiley.

Donella H. Meadows. 2008. *Thinking in Systems*. Chelsea Green.

Peter Merholz and Kristin Skinner. 2016. *Org Design for Design Orgs: Building and Managing In-House Design Teams*. O'Reilly Media.

Jeff Patton with Peter Economy. 2014. *User Story Mapping: Discover the Whole Story, Build the Right Product*. O'Reilly Media.

Melissa Perri. 2018. *Escaping the Build Trip: How Effective Product Management Creates Real Value*. O'Reilly Media.

Theodore M. Porter. 2020. *Trust in Numbers: The Pursuit of Objectivity in Science and Public Life*, 2nd edition. Princeton University Press.

James C. Scott. 2020. *Seeing Like a State: How Certain Schemes to Improve the Human Condition Have Failed*. Yale University Press.

Josh Seiden. 2019. *Outcomes Over Output: Why Customer Behavior is the Key Metric for Business Success*. Sense & Respond Press.

Matthew Skelton and Manuel Païs. 2019. *Team Topologies: Organizing Business and Technology Teams for Fast Flow*. IT Revolution Press.

On government, public service and civic tech

Hilary Cottam. 2019. *Radical Help: How We Can Remake the Relationships between Us and Revolutionise the Welfare State*. Virago.

Tara Dawson-McGuiness and Hana Schank. 2021. *Power to the Public: The Promise of Public Interest Technology*. Princeton University Press.

Cyd Harrell. 2020. *A Civic Technologist's Practice Guide*. Five Seven Five Books.

Ryan Ko. 2020. Renewed principles of delivery-driven government (https://codeforamerica.org/news/ renewed-principles-of-delivery-driven-government/).

Julian Le Grand. 2006. *Motivation, Agency, and Public Policy: Of Knights and Knaves, Pawns and Queens*. Oxford University Press.

Jennifer Pahlka. 2018. Delivery-driven government: principles and practices for government in the digital age (https://medium.com/ code-for-america/delivery-driven-government-67e698c57c7b).

Jennifer Pahlka. 2023. *Recoding America: Why Government Is Failing in the Digital Age and How We Can Do Better*. Macmillan.

James Plunkett. 2021. *End State: 9 Ways Society is Broken – And How We Can Fix It*. Orion Publishing Group.

John Seddon. 2008. *Systems Thinking in the Public Sector: The Failure of the Reform Regime … And a Manifesto for a Better Way*. Triarchy Press.

Working together and communicating

Russell Davies. 2021. *Everything I Know about Life I Learned from Powerpoint*. Profile Books.

Rob Fitzpatrick. 2019. *The Workshop Survival Guide: How to Design and Teach Educational Workshops that Work Every Time*. Independently Published.

Dave Gray. 2016. *Liminal Thinking: Create the Change You Want by Changing the Way You Think*. Rosenfeld Media.

Marshall B. Rosenberg. 2015. *Nonviolent Communication – A Language of Life: Life-Changing Tools for Healthy Relationships*. Puddle Dancer Press.

Giles Turnbull. 2021. *The Agile Comms Handbook*. Use the Human Voice Ltd.

Chris Voss with Tahl Raz. 2016. *Never Split the Difference: Negotiating as if Your Life Depended on It*. Cornerstone Digital.

Emily Webber. 2016. *Building Successful Communities of Practice: Discover How Connecting People Makes Better Organisations*. Blurb.

On building better tools, products and services

Lou Downe. 2021. *Good Services: How to Design Services that Work*. BIS Publishers.

Sarah Drummond. 2022. Full stack service design. http://sarah-drummond.com/full-stack-service-design/.

Erika Hall. 2013. *Just Enough Research*. A Book Apart.

Sarah Richards. 2017. *Content Design*. Independently Published.

Kathy Sierra. 2015. *Badass: Making Users Awesome*. O'Reilly Media.

Acknowledgements

Infinite appreciation is due to everyone that has shaped my thinking, shared their time and ideas, and enabled me to write this book.

The people I could and should thank are far too numerous to mention individually, but I wanted to especially thank the legends that are Tom Loosemore (who also nudged me into writing this book), Matti Keltanen, Lara Sampson and Andrew Greenway and to credit the many ideas, concepts and suggestions they have generously shared and contributed over the years. Huge respect to the brilliant team at Public Digital, of which Tom, Lara and Andrew are partners.

A big thank you to everyone who shared their work and experiences so openly and generously for this book, to help us all raise our game: Katy Arnold, Deb Boore, Jeanette Clement, Cathy Dutton, Philippa Elworthy, Colin Foley, Rohan Gye, Kylie Havelock, Rachel Hope, Eileen Logie, Lynne Roberts, James Spirit, Jo Straw, Rob Thompson, Tero Väänänen, Conor Ward, Pete Ward, Alice Whitehead and Melissa Witte.

I owe much gratitude to the many others who initiated – and who significantly contribute to – our collective thinking and knowledge about services.

Thank you in particular to Mike Bracken, and to many other friends and family, especially Alex, Nicky and Liz. Enormous gratitude for my Mum, Hellan, who would encourage us all to be the boldest version of ourselves (as well as to shake things up). And thanks to my Dad, Julian, and Lynda for all their practical help.

Many thanks to my editor Sam Clark, and for earlier editing by Owen Gregory. And to Matt Howard, who created the illustrations, and Emyr Cummins, who designed the book cover.

I am also very grateful to all the early readers, contributors and supporters, particularly Honey Dacanay, Johanna Kollmann, Liam Hawkes, Amelia Austin, Andrew Knight and Jeanette Clement.

And thanks to you

Thank you for all your effort in helping our organizations and institutions make better services for us all, and thanks for reading this book. I hope that at least some of it helps you to create more supportive conditions inside the organizations you work with and for.

Endnotes

Preface

1   Quoted from a conversation with Matti Keltanen and shared with his permission.

Introduction

1   https://www.computerworld.com/article/3645372/what-apples-approach-to-building-services-income-tells-us.html.

2   https://hbr.org/2018/05/how-ford-is-thinking-about-the-future.

3   https://ee.co.uk/.

4   Shared with permission from Leisa Reichelt: https://www.disambiguity.com/help-joy-help-you/.

5   https://hbr.org/2007/05/silo-busting-how-to-execute-on-the-promise-of-customer-focus.

6   https://www.belfercenter.org/publication/government-tech-projects-fail-default-it-doesnt-have-be-way.

Chapter 1

1   Lou Downe, *Good Services: How to Design Services that Work* (BIS Publishers, 2021).

2   Lou Downe: https://designnotes.blog.gov.uk/2015/06/22/good-services-are-verbs-2/.

3   https://smartstart.services.govt.nz/.

4   https://www.natwest.com/mortgages/first-time-buyers/first-time-buyer-guide.html.

5   https://design-system.service.gov.uk/patterns/step-by-step-navigation/.

6   https://gds.blog.gov.uk/2015/07/13/lets-talk-about-permissions/.

7   https://www.gov.uk/government/publications/roadmap-for-digital-
    and-data-2022-to-2025/transforming-for-a-digital-future-2022-to-2025-
    roadmap-for-digital-and-data#annex; https://www.gov.uk/service-
    manual/design/create-a-list-of-services; https://ukhomeoffice.github.
    io/coe/service-list/.

8   https://public.digital/2022/01/21/what-does-working-in-the-
    open-mean.

9   https://dfedigital.blog.gov.uk/2021/03/04/service-line-
    mapping/; https://hodigital.blog.gov.uk/2018/06/07/creating-
    a-list-of-services/; https://mojdigital.blog.gov.uk/2019/06/06/
    building-a-register-of-public-facing-services/.

10 https://www.redcross.org.uk/; a conversation with Jo Straw in May
    2022; https://medium.com/digital-and-innovation-at-british-red-cross/
    weve-created-a-list-of-services-now-what-cf60921609c3.

11 https://www.boxt.co.uk/.

Chapter 2

1   https://gds.blog.gov.uk/2015/08/18/mapping-new-ideas-for-
    the-digital-justice-system-2/.

2   Service Canada: https://www.theguardian.com/society/
    transformationalgovernment/story/0,,2021777,00.html;
    https://www.canada.ca/en/revenue-agency/services/tax/individuals/
    life-events.html.

3   https://codeforamerica.org/programs/social-safety-net/food-
    benefits/; https://snapstories.codeforamerica.org/.

4   http://sarah-drummond.com/full-stack-service-design/.

5   See the following series of Twitter posts by Kim Goodwin:
    https://twitter.com/kimgoodwin/status/1389772636218019842.

6   See the following tweet from Caroline Jarret: https://twitter.com/
    cjforms/status/485001003226648577.

7   *Just Enough Research* by Erika Hall (2nd edition, 2019, A Book
    Apart); *Interviewing for Research* by Andrew Travers (2013, https://
    andrewtravers.co/book); *Validating Product Ideas* by Tomer Sharon
    (2016, https://rosenfeldmedia.com/books/lean-user-research).

8   Quoted from conversation and email discussion with Colin Foley
    May–June 2022.

9   Adapted from emails with Jeanette Clement in April
    2022 and from https://medium.com/bts-design-team/

how-we-are-using-service-patterns-to-improve-efficiency-at-bt-ee-f9ac2dcdccc6.

10 Conversation with Alice Whitehead (service owner for funding, DLUHC), June 2022.

11 https://supportingfamilies.blog.gov.uk/2021/05/21/rebuilding-resilience-a-familys-journey/.

Chapter 3

1 https://beyondcommandandcontrol.com/failure-demand/.

2 https://en.wikipedia.org/wiki/Psychological_contract; https://www.slideshare.net/cxpartners/designing-for-delight-giles-colborne.

3 Peter Drucker. 1993. *Management: Tasks, Responsibilities, Practices*, reprint edition. Harper Business.

4 https://tsharon.medium.com/measuring-task-success-6ed2ffba9eee.

5 https://www.howtomeasureanything.com/.

6 https://www.gov.uk/service-manual/service-standard.

7 Shared with permission from the Home Office and drawing on content from https://services.blog.gov.uk/2021/03/05/showing-the-rewards-of-user-centred-service-design-at-scale/.

8 Quoted from conversation and email discussion with Colin Foley May–June 2022.

9 https://www.localgov.co.uk/three-councils-to-test-simplified-planning-apps/52551.

10 https://peekvision.org/; also quoted from email discussion with Melissa Witte (Peek Vision leadership), May 2022.

Chapter 4

1 https://hbr.org/2015/04/a-process-for-empathetic-product-design; https://www.slideshare.net/katetarling/the-actual-problems-to-be-solved & https://hollidazed.co.uk/2015/07/28/frame-the-problem/.

2 https://www.notifications.service.gov.uk/; https://www.payments.service.gov.uk/.

3 https://teamtopologies.com/key-concepts-content/finding-good-stream-boundaries-with-independent-service-heuristics.

4 https://playbook.hackney.gov.uk/tech-radar/.

5 Quoted from interview with Rohan Gye in August 2022.

6   https://www.technologyreview.com/2021/03/17/1020811/
    better-tech-government-pandemic-united-states/.

7   https://www.mahindrafinance.com/.

8   https://hbr.org/2019/09/put-purpose-at-the-core-of-your-strategy.

Chapter 5

1   https://publicpolicydesign.blog.gov.uk/2021/10/21/innovating-public-
    services-at-scale/.

2   https://publicpolicydesign.blog.gov.uk/.

3   https://twitter.com/jamestplunkett.

4   https://twitter.com/catdrew.

5   https://en.digst.dk/digital-governance/digital-ready-legislation/
    what-is-digital-ready-legislation/.

6   https://en.digst.dk/digital-governance/digital-ready-legislation/what-
    is-digital-ready-legislation/; https://en.digst.dk/digital-governance/
    digital-ready-legislation/guidances-and-tools/; https://en.digst.dk/
    digital-governance/digital-architecture/.

7   Quoted from interview with Rachel Hope and Pete Ward in July 2022.

8   Quoted from interview with Rohan Gye in August 2022.

Chapter 6

1   Richard Rumelt. 2011. *Good Strategy, Bad Strategy*. Profile Books. See
    also https://www.annashipman.co.uk/jfdi/russells-strategy-advice.
    html.

2   https://twitter.com/larasampson.

3   Lara Sampson in *Lessons from Lockdown* (Said Business School,
    University of Oxford); see also https://www.youtube.com/
    watch?v=-BFV2Kof6N4&t=1038s.

4   See the book *Sense and Respond* by Jeff Gothelf and Josh Seidenbook
    (https://jeffgothelf.com/books/#sense-respond).

5   https://www.bbva.com/en/the-importance-of-customer-journeys-
    in-banking/; https://www.bbva.com/en/path-digital-transformation-
    series-pillar-1-reinvent-consumer-journey/.

6   https://www.bbva.com/en/bbva-compass-express-personal-loan-
    goes-digital-opens-consumers-multiple-states/.

7   https://www.gov.uk/guidance/get-a-discount-with-the-eat-
    out-to-help-out-scheme.

8 https://blog.wearefuturegov.com/citizens-portals-y-n-42e57fad2874.

9 Quoted from email discussion with Eileen Logie, May 2022.

10 Quoted from conversation and email discussion with Deb Boore, May 2022.

Chapter 7

1 https://teamtopologies.com/.

2 https://design-system.service.gov.uk/.

3 https://www.payments.service.gov.uk/.

4 https://www.notifications.service.gov.uk/.

5 https://federal-field-notes.ca/articles/2021-06-21-you-dont-need-a-platform-you-need-one-thing-that-works/.

6 https://en.wikipedia.org/wiki/Werner_Vogels.

7 John Seddon. 2014. *The Whitehall Effect*. Triarchy Press. John Seddon. 2008. *Systems Thinking in the Public Sector*, Triarchy Press. John Seddon. 2017. *Beyond Command and Control*. Routledge.

8 https://en.wikipedia.org/wiki/Experience_curve_effects.

9 https://reform.uk/wp-content/uploads/2021/01/210114-Digital-public-services-final-final.pdf-1_0.pdf.

10 Quoted from email discussion with Tero Väänänen in June 2022.

Chapter 8

1 https://socitm.net/.

2 https://www.effortmark.co.uk/useful-usable-used-new-look-council-website/.

3 http://theleanstartup.com/.

4 https://www.prodpad.com/blog/the-birth-of-the-modern-roadmap/.

5 https://cutlefish.substack.com/p/tbm-41b52-suitably-detailed-roadmap.

6 https://www.jpattonassociates.com/story-mapping/.

7 https://blog.mattedgar.com/2015/01/23/the-last-target-operating-model-youll-ever-need/.

8 https://twitter.com/larasampson.

9 http://technogoggles.com/2022/03/20/prioritising-in-gov/.

10 Conversation with James Spirit (head of product, NHS England) on 31 May 2022; see also https://digital.nhs.uk/features/a-vital-injection.

11 Quoted from conversation and email discussion with Deb Boore, May 2022.

Chapter 9

1 https://hbr.org/2007/05/silo-busting-how-to-execute-on-the-promise-of-customer-focus.

2 https://www.gov.uk/service-manual/the-team/what-each-role-does-in-service-team.

3 https://emilywebber.co.uk/building-successful-communities-of-practice/; http://strongdesignbook.com/.

4 https://www.gov.uk/service-manual/design/working-across-organisational-boundaries.

5 https://medium.com/@ctdesign/designing-caseworking-systems-2-4d3efd1fbf82.

6 Quoted from conversation and email discussion with Colin Foley May–June 2022.

7 Quoted from interview with Eileen Logie (former deputy director, ESFA, and service owner of the Apprenticeship Service) on 19 May 2022.

8 Quoted from conversation and email discussion with Deb Boore, May 2022.

9 Shared with permission from https://wearecitizensadvice.org.uk/what-we-learned-from-our-first-energy-hack-day-2c177be4d8e7.

Chapter 10

1 Lara Sampson presentation: https://twitter.com/NavaPBC/status/1509203694486700032.

2 https://www.standishgroup.com/sample_research_files/Haze4.pdf.

3 https://www.prince2.com/uk/blog/project-vs-programme.

4 Quoted from Twitter, June 2022: https://twitter.com/e17chrisfleming/status/1541836731082743808?s=20&t=fND66udzHOBXY6x2xgvHKQ.

5 https://www.gov.uk/service-manual/service-assessments.

6 Quoted from conversation and email discussion with Kylie Havelock, May 2022.

Chapter 11

1 https://www.gov.uk/service-manual/agile-delivery.

2 https://www.gov.uk/service-manual/agile-delivery/how-the-discovery-phase-works.

3 Quoted from conversation and email discussion with Colin Foley May–June 2022.

4 Conversation and email discussion with Katy Arnold February–May 2022.

5 Quoted from conversation and email discussion with Deb Boore, May 2022.

6 Quoted from interview with Rachel Hope and Pete Ward in July 2022.

Chapter 12

1 http://www.russelldavies.com/powerpoint; https://agilecommshandbook.com/.

2 https://senseandrespond.co/.

3 https://www.gov.uk/government/publications/roadmap-for-digital-and-data-2022-to-2025/transforming-for-a-digital-future-2022-to-2025-roadmap-for-digital-and-data.

Chapter 13

1 Shared by Andrew Greenway in an email conversation of 31 May 2022.

2 https://www.bcg.com/publications/2021/fixing-digital-funding-in-government.

3 Thanks to Andrew Greenway for his insight on funding models and workarounds.

4 https://public.digital/2021/02/09/funding-digital-government-initiatives; https://www.bcg.com/publications/2021/fixing-digital-funding-in-government.

5 https://www.gov.uk/service-manual/agile-delivery/spend-controls-pipeline-process.

6 Thanks to the anonymous respondents to a questionnaire circulated in August/September 2022 on social media about tips for working around financial constraints in large organizations. The responses included this suggestion.

7 https://avfletcher.medium.com/bau-doesnt-have-to-be-bau-23480f095aa0.

8   https://katetarling.com/2022/11/03/the-drivers-of-digital/.

9   https://en.wikipedia.org/wiki/Conway%27s_law.

10 https://ntouk.wordpress.com/2017/02/09/re-engineer-government-abolish-government-departments/.

11 https://mojdigital.blog.gov.uk/2022/02/04/sum-of-all-the-strategies/; https://www.nytimes.com/2021/11/24/technology/government-tech.html.

12 Quoted from interview with Conor Ward in June 2022.

13 Quoted from conversation and email discussion with Colin Foley May–June 2022.

14 From email discussion with Rob Thompson and Katy Arnold in June 2022.

15 From email discussion with Lynne Roberts and Cathy Dutton in May 2022 and taken from https://defradigital.blog.gov.uk/2021/09/06/building-a-team-to-design-defra-services/.